The Downers . . . have a marriage that will be a blessing to the family for generations to come . . . a legacy of love, honor, productivity and fun! Anyone who'd like to have a marriage like that should read *Optimize Your Marriage*.

rong
:ader
rado

Phil Downer is a "man's man... ...us the rare combination of military toughness with genuine tenderness. He communicates through his books and speaking equally well. His books are full of practical, biblical principles and are fun to read. People who read and hear him experience life changes. In a day calling for integrity, Phil fills the bill.

Dr. Bob Horner
senior pastor, Peachtree Corners Baptist Church,
Norcross, Georgia

This is not another "how to" book. Phil and Susy have "done it." They have been honest, open and transparent in sharing their failures and successes as both spouses and parents. Their children are the evidence of their godly parenting. What a remarkable testimony! Their lives represent biblical principles put into action. God is truly blessing the fruit of their labor as a result of their obedience to His Word.

Don Mitchell
chairman of the board, CBMC International
former executive, General Motors

I cannot overemphasize how blessed my husband and I were by reading *Optimize Your Marriage*. This would be a wonderful book to do with another couple for mentoring. I also have to admit how very much we learned from it. . . . The thing that comes shining through is how willing Phil and Susy are to let God work, shape and mold them. That's tough. I laughed out loud many times over certain experiences they had; I could definitely relate to them. I underlined and highlighted, and Don and I have discussed many things.

Nina Mitchell
wife, mother and grandmother

OPTIMIZE *Your Marriage*

MAKING AN **ETERNAL IMPACT** ON FAMILY AND FRIENDS

PHIL & SUSY DOWNER
with Ken Walker

✠ CHRISTIAN PUBLICATIONS, INC.
CAMP HILL, PENNSYLVANIA

✠CHRISTIAN PUBLICATIONS, INC.
3825 Hartzdale Drive, Camp Hill, PA 17011
www.christianpublications.com

Faithful, biblical publishing since 1883

Optimize Your Marriage
ISBN: 0-88965-216-3
© 2003 by Phil and Susy Downer
LOC Control Number: 2003105132
All rights reserved
Printed in the United States of America

04   05   06   07   5   4   3   2

CONTENTS

FOREWORD

If Phil Downer had lived at the time of King David he would have been the leader of David's "thirty mighty men." This soldier's consuming passion is to walk with integrity with the Lord. He strives to develop greater humility in his marriage and family and to be available to God to disciple his children and those to whom he and Susy minister.

Susy, as an experienced and successful attorney with Delta Air Lines, made a large leap of faith, resigning her position as a corporate officer of a major airline to devote full-time attention to their family. Later that family would grow to six children and the expanding ministry that God has brought them. Susy is one of those courageous, modern-day Ruths who overcame the barrenness of a broken marriage and bravely followed the Lord's leading to leave the familiar land of her legal career and step out in faith in full-time parenting, educating and ministering out of the home. Perhaps her most courageous challenge was staying in a broken marriage until God reached her husband and answered her prayer for a new, God-centered marriage full of love, affection and intimacy.

It is a privilege to call Phil and Susy my friends, to witness firsthand and from a distance the fruitfulness of their lives that can only be attributed to our Lord Jesus Christ's handiwork in broken and contrite vessels. Perhaps one of the things most effective about Phil and Susy's extensive writing and speaking ministries is their willingness to be utterly transparent and open with their failures, challenges, hurts and fears. They often relate how God has made a difference in their lives and used that difference to impact other people in many lands. It is a privilege to serve as chairman of their endorsement committee and I commend their ministry to you.

Pat Morley
president, Man in the Mirror Ministries
author of *Man in the Mirror*
president, National Coalition of Men's Ministries

INTRODUCTION

Susy: The question "How can I continue to live with a man I don't love?" raced through my mind as Phil and I endured continuing conflict in our marriage. I was a Christian now; so was Phil. But I had lost the joy, enthusiasm, warmth, commitment and love I felt at the altar. All had been stolen by our conflict, his anger and stubbornness, the crush of our careers and, frankly, my independence.

Phil: When I met Susy I had found the woman of my dreams. She loved to embrace when I dropped her off after a dinner date. She was my pure and lovely fiancée with whom I intended to live happily for the rest of my life. But, after surviving combat in Vietnam, I brought my hard-charging, prideful attitude into our marriage. Very quickly, my pompous, self-serving, domineering ways crushed Susy's heart. After marriage, her warm embraces turned to indifference. Though my anger caused this change, I thought I had been defrauded.

Susy: Defrauded? Here I was, a faithful wife, wondering what happened to the Prince Charming who always seemed to have my best interests at heart. What happened to the gentleman with whom I never had even one argument during courtship? It seemed like he was taking all the pain of childhood and marine combat experience out on me. Year after year I was suffering for pain caused by other people I didn't even know! All I wanted to do was live in harmony or get out. I couldn't face living the rest of my life married to someone I didn't love.

1

Had we not had godly people discipling us—a doctor meeting with Phil; a young mother whose husband had deserted her meeting with me—we never would have made it. We would have become another one of those sad divorce statistics you hear about so often. The difference was that our mentors convinced us that with God nothing was impossible, even the healing of our disastrous marriage.

Maybe you are looking for personally enriching and deepening soil. Please believe us: Even a lukewarm marriage can become an exciting, fruitful, joyful and intimate relationship from which will spring children who can truly make a difference in our world.

As we became convinced that the spiritual parenting from which we had benefitted had set the course of our lives, we focused on the need to raise children who would be free of pain, sin and brokenness. We wanted them equipped for adulthood without the generational carnage we brought into our marriage. As Phil and I say repeatedly, if *our* marriage can be saved, there isn't one beyond God's healing touch. There is no marriage that is rocking along in neutral that can't become the best you've ever dreamed of. Phil and I are best friends and very much in love today. What a miracle!

Phil: Thankfully, with God's intervention, we reconciled our differences with Him and each other and lived to talk about it. We take great satisfaction in persuading other couples that mutual irritation and disagreements don't doom them to divorce court or a stale existence.

Although we both have law degrees, our expertise in marriage and family relationships comes solely from experience and seeking God, individually and with other people. Our "hard knocks" education has spanned three decades and many challenges. These principles have been the bedrock of our one-on-one and couples discipleship ministry and the focus of our speaking at conferences and retreats through Discipleship Network of America.

It isn't easy staying married in this society. Every week I hear another sad tale of a marriage gone awry. This isn't just among twenty-something couples, many of whom were raised to treat divorce as an acceptable way of resolving differences. The ones that make my stomach churn most are the breakups after twenty, twenty-five or thirty-five years, often involving people in the church. Claims that Jesus has the answers to life's problems ring hollow when non-Christians inspect our faltering homes and relationships.

Susy and I realize we can't turn around this disturbing trend on our own. But *Optimize Your Marriage* is our effort to make a difference. Just staying together for the sake of the kids won't bring you happiness; it may ultimately leave you disillusioned and bitter. The suggestions we offer in this book on how to have a more joyful marriage are tested in the fire of experience. Since we are happier today than we were at the altar, we know that it is possible to grow—and glow. Within these pages we also look at such issues as dealing with anger, healing past hurts, sexual purity, communication and how to pass God's truth and ways on to our children.

Marriage is more than resolving personal differences with your mate. We also discuss how to instill a deep, Christ-centered relationship within your children. It isn't easy. Nothing worth having comes without applying some elbow grease to the situation. Still, we have seen how these efforts can bloom in adolescence, thrive in the teenage years and literally change the future. If you have toddlers scampering across the rug and threatening your sanity, you may not be thinking much about tomorrow. But the future will become more important with each passing year. And, if your children are older, it's never too late to build closer relationships of love and influence. A vision for family ministry today can reap contented, well-adjusted children who go on to become healthy, well-adjusted parents. We welcome you to join us on the journey.

Chapter One
MINDING THE HOME

———— Phil Downer

We called him "General George Patton," but not because he was a rugged, courageous warrior. The nickname mocked his character. Calling this guy the famed American hero was like comparing a Volkswagen minibus to a 747 jet airplane.

This George symbolized everything you didn't want in a United States Marine. Lazy and incompetent, he proved that sometimes even the toughest trainers can't transform a shiftless, slothful, lackadaisical man into a lean, mean fighting machine. If our George Patton covered your back, better turn around a lot to make sure you were still alive.

It sounds funny today, but it wasn't in the rice paddies of Vietnam. We didn't find anything amusing about a marine who didn't carry his weight. Particularly the night my company selected nine of us for jungle patrol. (A company consists of 120 marines.) That day we had moved out as a large force in enemy territory.

We went through a long series of movements. We maneuvered through open fields, hit tree lines and moved on. We didn't suffer any casualties, nor did we inflict many. But

5

our plan included selecting a small group for drop-off patrol. Nine men would hide in the jungle until nightfall. Dividing into three teams of three men each, we set up an L-shaped ambush. The machine gunner sat on the pivot. As the enemy closed in under cover of darkness, we would spring a surprise attack.

This night I took the pivot with two other men, including our ill-named hero. The pivot man triggered the ambush. Notice I said pivot "man" instead of men. Even in the most dangerous situation, after a day of tromping through combat, marines need sleep. The deep darkness lasted for about six hours. Our nighttime schedule called for two hours of sleep and an hour on watch. It wasn't the best arrangement for resting, but at least you got some shut-eye, which is what I was doing when General Patton took over as sentry.

> # Calling this guy "General George Patton" was like comparing a Volkswagen minibus to a 747 jet airplane.

It didn't take much combat to learn to sleep lightly. That night in the midst of my catnap, I suddenly woke up. Looking around, I wondered why I felt so uneasy. Then I saw him. Sure enough—George was snoozing! The very man standing watch in the key position, responsible for setting off a chain of events designed to defeat the enemy!

We were encamped in heavy enemy territory near the Ho Chi Minh Trail, so maybe you can understand my flash of anger. Grabbing my M-16, I rammed the gun's butt into the base of his neck. It called for careful aim. But if you knew how to use your weapon, it was an extremely effective method of waking somebody up without breaking his neck or any bones.

It knocked the breath out of him too. A real attention grabber. George had endangered every man's life on patrol and those of the covering troops behind us. If the enemy picked us off, they could have sneaked up on the rest and caused serious damage.

Not long after George came to his senses, we pulled out, thankfully without losing a man because of George's failure to stand watch.

Yet what stands out in my mind from those days isn't only the harrowing flights to safety, the thick air that made it feel like we were fighting in a steam bath or the sleep-deprived nights on jungle patrol. No, it was also our General Patton shirking his duty behind enemy lines. Charged with the obligation of leading an attack and caring for those around him, he sat down and went to sleep.

The Need for Watchmen

The battle we face in twenty-first-century America is far more significant, precious and life-threatening than any conflict I faced in Vietnam. We're engaged in a struggle for eternity, one which vitally concerns the future of our children, grandchildren, nieces and nephews. This fight will affect each of our communities and our nation.

Yet too many of us are asleep at the switch. Like the man who risked dozens of lives in combat, we snooze while the enemy attacks and overcomes many of our fellow soldiers.

A watchman sounds the alarm. There are many areas where we can impact the world through vigilant action in daily life. Take, for instance, someone willing to sound the alarm for a friend. How many of your friends have experienced personal problems such as the collapse of their marriage because of an affair or an addiction to alcohol or pornography?

I grieve over the pastors, famous Christians and personal acquaintances who have fallen in recent years. It seems each month brings another revelation of divorce, adultery or chaos in Christians' lives. Some people, wishing to be loving and forgiving, gently encourage these Christians with letters of condolence or personal greetings. That is a bit late. Better that someone sound the alarm *before* it is too late.

I am part of an accountability group. Every Christian should make an effort to join one. Lay yourself open to others and allow them to ask you tough questions. It will help you see your blind spots and shortcomings. This falls under the category of "minding the home." Whether you live in suburbia or the inner city, the home that matters isn't measured by square footage. It's the caring relationships under the roof that matter.

Once a member of my group got concerned about my travel schedule and its impact on my family life. Even though I often take my family along, that isn't always possible. As we chatted, Scott asked, "Phil, how much are you traveling?"

"Quite a bit," I replied. (That's lawyerese for, "I don't want to tell you.")

"Well, how much?"

"Quite a bit," I repeated.

"Are you getting any time with Susy?" he asked.

"Of course," I said, relating an old story about a friend advising me to date my wife. I had done that faithfully ever since. But when I gave that answer, he pressed further. "I'm talking about time alone, where you're off alone with just

her and spending time with her. When's the last time you
had a week alone?"

"We've done that," I said defensively.

"When's the last time you had a week alone?"

I squirmed, feeling like the room was overheating.

"Do you think it would be a good idea to have a week
alone with your wife?"

> "His watchmen are blind, all of
> them know nothing. All of them are
> mute dogs unable to bark, dreamers
> lying down, who love to slumber;
> and the dogs are greedy, they are not
> satisfied. And they are shepherds who
> have no understanding; they have all
> turned to their own way, each one
> to his unjust gain, to the last one."
> —Isaiah 56:10-11

"Yeah, I think it probably would," I said, grateful when the
discussion moved on to other topics. But the next time we
met, he asked about it again. I tried giving another evasive answer, but he demanded to see my calendar. He told me to get
it out and show him where I had planned our getaway.

I don't know that I've ever felt more awkward. He forced
me to confess I hadn't followed through on his suggestion.
Thanks to Scott and other men in that group, today my
wife and I get away once a year for rest and relaxation.

What a blessing! And it happened because some men came
alongside and acted as caring overseers. They sounded the

alarm before the enemy sneaked in to wreak havoc. He can attack any of us through stress, too much time away from family or creating emotional distance from our spouse.

Like tides against the shoreline, the latter has eroded millions of marriages. Ultimately, the responsibility belongs to the couple. Still, more of us need to be the kind of watchmen who will sound the alarm for our friends and colleagues.

I formerly served as the leader of a businessmen's ministry. The night of my installation in office, they held a late-night reception at the hotel. Everyone excitedly patted me on the back, wanted to know more about me and asked questions about my plans for the future. Finally the crowd dwindled to a few people. I got involved in a long conversation with one of my spiritual mentors.

He talked about the privilege of what I was getting to do. "You better not blow it," he warned. "You've got to be careful with women. You've got to be careful with your integrity."

I replied that I had a daily quiet time and listed the things I did to avoid trouble. I assured him I didn't travel with women, didn't leave hotels to cruise around town alone and didn't counsel women in one-on-one sessions. I told him about my accountability group and how Susy and I also held each other accountable. I hoped that would wrap up our talk. It was past midnight and I'm an early riser.

Instead he repeated his advice. "Phil, you've got just one chance at this. If you blow it, you're gone. You just can't blow it. You've got to be careful. There are a lot of people counting on you."

He went on for fifteen or twenty minutes longer, prodding, counseling, warning and encouraging. Obviously he wasn't in awe of me or the position for which I had been chosen. He felt great concern that I do everything possible to maintain my personal purity and close relationship with the Lord.

Tough Questions

When is the last time you faced some tough questions? If more leaders in high places had faced some tough questions, how many could have been saved from disgrace over the past twenty years? How many divorces could have been avoided? How many children would be happy, well-adjusted, productive adults instead of coping with the pain of a broken home? How much brighter would Christians' light shine?

> "But if the watchman sees the sword coming and does not blow the trumpet and the people are not warned, and a sword comes and takes a person from them, he is taken away in his iniquity; but his blood I will require from the watchman's hand."
> —Ezekiel 33:6

We often don't welcome encounters like I had that night in the hotel. Without a humble spirit we can get our noses out of joint. *Who does he think he is, asking me such personal questions? Doesn't he know I've been faithful to my spouse for twenty years? Doesn't he know I'm a leader in my church? Doesn't he know I would never do anything like that?*

This isn't the correct attitude. As Galatians 6:1 warns, "Brethren, even if anyone is caught in any trespass, you who are spiritual, restore such a one in a spirit of gentleness; each one looking to yourself, *so that you too will not be tempted.*"

Not long ago, that late-night session came back to my mind. While traveling, I broke a zipper on my suitcase. I went down to the hotel lobby to get some tape to repair it. As soon as I got there, a woman walked up to me.

"Hi," she said, smiling. After I returned her greeting, she said, "I'm a Malaysian airline attendant and I would like you to come up to my room tonight. Right now. The room number is 905. I've got a roommate. If she's there, we'll go to your room. What's your room number?"

I don't know whether I said anything. All I remember is turning on my heels and running. Some men had warned me about this very possibility. My mentor's advice rang in my ears: "You only get one chance. Don't blow it. A lot of people are counting on you."

How grateful I am for the men and women who have told Susy and me what we need to hear instead of praising us constantly. Two points are worth noting about that hotel encounter:

First, in addition to the counsel from spiritual instructors, I had a biblical model to follow. When Joseph faced enticing advances from his master's wife, he resisted:

> As she spoke to Joseph day after day, he did not listen to her to lie beside her or be with her. Now it happened one day that he went into the house to do his work, and none of the men of the household was there inside. She caught him by his garment, saying, "Lie with me!" And he left his garment in her hand and fled, and went outside. (Genesis 39:10-12)

Joseph didn't try to act like a spiritual giant who could withstand powerful temptation. He knew if he didn't run he would fall.

Second, because I had an accountability group back home, I knew they were going to ask me about my trip. Questions like, "Where did you go? What did you do? Did any women make advances toward you? What happened?" I knew I couldn't face them and keep up a false front for very long. Sooner or later I would crumble and have to clean up the mess. Far better to avoid the mess.

This is the kind of thing we need to do with our spouse, friends and children. We must invest in their lives and warn them of potential trouble. Men love to pour themselves into building corporations, institutions and other endeavors. But many neglect their duty to build up the most important resource of all—the people around them. Homes are built of loved ones, not bricks.

> I was shocked to see an intelligent, attractive young woman on a mission trip looking at pornographic material. The pictures were so offensive I had to quickly avert my eyes. This is a good example of young people's need for mentors to help them mind their spiritual houses.

As a practical course of action, try getting involved with a young couple who struggle to keep going. The kind who fight to put food on the table, pay the bills, deal with work pressures and keep the kids in line. Or with high school and college students who need direction. Why not take time to put up with music you would rather not hear and deal with

culture shock you'd prefer to avoid so you can speak into
their lives?

I saw the crying need to deal with teens on a trip a few
years ago. On the airplane, I sat next to a young woman who
was taking a mission trip with a high school group. Her
friends were passing a book around, taking turns reading it,
laughing and pointing. When the book got to her, I took a
quick glance and immediately turned away.

I had made a commitment not to let my eyes fall on anything that would cause me to lust. The autobiography of a
professional athlete, this book was crammed with such material. Yet here sat an attractive, well-mannered young woman
(on a mission trip!) reading this kind of trash. And laughing
about it. She and her friends lacked a watchman to warn them
of such dangers.

Isn't it worth getting a little uncomfortable to pass on
godly values to young people? Would you rather remain silent while they parade around wearing T-shirts that bear the
names of negative role models or obscene sayings? None of
us care for teens emulating people who stand for the opposite
of what we believe. But unless we're willing to take a step and
speak to them, guess who will have the most influence?

Seeking the Lost

Going after the lost is another worthy pursuit for those
who want to see strong homes built in our nation.

The idea of talking with strangers may scare you to
death. You may think, *What will I say? How will I answer
their questions? What if they brush me off?*

The secret is to look for opportunities to speak with someone who may be more receptive than you can imagine. Naturally you can't carry on a leisurely conversation with someone

behind a fast-food counter who has a dozen customers in line. But don't be so insensitive you miss wide-open doors.

My natural dislike for a rude salesman almost caused me to miss such an opportunity. It happened on a dream vacation to Hawaii. Susy and I were browsing in shops on an island and walked into a chart shop. Hanging on the walls were old documents, charts and English indentures, all framed and very expensive.

While we enjoyed looking at these artifacts, I didn't care for the salesman. Ever have someone get in your face and raise the hackles on your neck? Coming over, he immediately started bossing us around. Then he started swearing and using God's name in vain. Susy looked at me, said, "I'm out of here," and headed for the door. Though tempted to follow, I hung back to talk to him. I asked where he was from.

> "Preach the word; be ready in season and out of season; reprove, rebuke, exhort, with great patience and instruction."
> —2 Timothy 4:2

"Oh, I'm from France," he said. "Viva la France. I'm a Frenchman and I hate Hawaii."

If he didn't like Maui, I knew this guy had problems.

"The French, they're so cultured and intelligent," he continued. "They're so civilized."

"Yeah, and they're humble too, aren't they?" I asked sarcastically.

Missing the point, he agreed. Though I couldn't stand his arrogance, I restrained my tongue. Instead of saying anything more, I slowly backed out the door and took Susy to dinner. When we sat down, I couldn't stop thinking about him. Soon I said, "Honey, I've got to go back and talk to that guy."

"You're crazy," she said. "He'll blow you out of that place. He's not interested. He couldn't care less."

"I know. But I just need to go back and talk to him."

I went back to that shop three times that week, without success. Finally I caught him when no one else was around.

"Listen," I said, "when's the last time somebody came to you with a piece of information that you needed just because they cared about you?"

"That's never happened," he replied. "I don't mean today. I mean it's never happened."

"Well, friend, I want to tell you something. I was just like you. I ruined my marriage. I was full of bitterness, anger and hatred. I took it out on people. I hated my job. I hated where I lived. I was miserable."

"I've ruined every relationship," he said, interrupting me. His eyes grew soft. "My wife divorced me. My kids are scattered here and there. I've ruined them all."

"Let me tell you, Jesus Christ died for you on the cross," I said. I explained the steps he could take to find peace with God. I couldn't believe how receptive this nasty-tongued, tart old Frenchman was to this message. I promised to send him some more material on the subject. Now, I can't tell you he fell on his knees and prayed to receive Christ. But from a zero on a scale of ten in spiritual interest, he went up a couple of notches.

Right after I walked out, a small woman who couldn't have weighed more than 100 pounds came running after me. I wondered if I had left my wallet behind. She called, "Thank you. Thank you. I work with that man."

"You do?" I asked, surprised because I didn't remember seeing her there.

"He's the most vile man," she said. "I've been praying for him every day. I just want to thank you for caring enough to tell him about Jesus Christ. I know you're a Christian because of what you did."

> The woman came running after me as I left the shop. After telling me what a vile man he was, she said, "I just want to thank you for caring enough to tell him about Jesus Christ. I know you're a Christian because of what you did."

Until we get to heaven, I may never learn what my overtures to that man accomplished. But his reaction and that woman's comments made my day. Even though our children weren't along on that trip, I made sure I told them what happened. They need to know their father doesn't just *think* sharing is a good idea—he *does* it. How can we expect young people to tell their peers about Christ if we don't?

Our nation has a crying need for individuals and couples who will model faithfulness to Christ, not only to teach their children, but for the good of our nation. A parachurch leader recently told me the greatest need ministries have is talented people. Imagine the benefits of midlife professionals and experienced retirees investing themselves in Christ-centered organizations. Our society gets hung up on money as if it's the only resource that matters. Mature servants of God are worth their weight in gold.

Making Young Disciples

A few years ago I read a disheartening survey in *USA Today*. A poll for the national newspaper found only thirty-seven percent of those questioned believed our country would be in good hands when the next generation grows up. That condemns our nation—and I don't mean the young people. If adults' confidence is that low, it reflects poorly on the parents and grandparents. They are the people responsible for training our children. The watchmen have been asleep. Not only do we need overseers to ward off disaster in our homes and marriages, but we also need adults who will teach God's ways to their offspring.

There was a time when we could rely on Sunday school teachers to drill youngsters in biblical basics. Our public schools taught character and responsibility. Television and movie producers followed a moral code. That is no longer true. If we expect institutions to disciple our children, we will be sadly disappointed.

Of course, it was never their job anyway. That task belongs to parents. The astonishing success of Tiger Woods is a good example of the value of parents discipling their children. How did he become the best golfer in the world? His father trained him. What if his father had left the job to someone else? How good would Tiger be if he had hacked around the course with duffers? But because his father had a vision for Tiger, his father schooled him and taught him good golf habits.

He mentored him on the golf course the same way that Paul mentored Timothy in his faith. Likewise, fathers and mothers can't rely on organizations to disciple their children spiritually. Godly educators will tell you the greatest need children have is for their parents to teach, train and encourage them.

Susy and I homeschool our children. I'm involved in this method for the same reason I wear running shoes for long-distance jogging. If I don't, I will beat up my feet. The shoes are tools to help me exercise. Similarly, home-schooling is a tool to accomplish a purpose.

We want to build spiritual reproducers. We are trying to be faithful to the instruction God gives in the sixth chapter of Deuteronomy. We feel we can't do that as effectively if they're at school and wrapped up in homework and extra-curricular activities twelve hours a day.

> "These words, which I am commanding you today, shall be on your heart. You shall teach [my commands] diligently to your sons and shall talk of them when you sit in your house and when you walk by the way and when you lie down and when you rise up."
> —Deuteronomy 6:6-7

We have already seen results. Our children are among our best friends, and our relationships are strong enough that we are willing to be accountable to each other. For example, one time on a trip to Asia, I called home to see how everyone was doing. When Paul, who was fourteen at the time, got on the phone, he asked, "Dad, how are you doing?" That may sound like a throwaway question, something like, "Having a nice day?" but because of our closeness, I knew what he was asking.

He didn't want to know if I felt good or was leading successful meetings. He meant, "How have you been doing in your walk with God? Have you been patient with other people? Have you been a joy to be around this week? Have you been faithful to Mom? Can all of us be proud of you while you're away from home?"

Each of us needs to be a servant to others, helping them to remain strong. We also need them by our side, caring for our souls, checking up on us and keeping us accountable. This is the eternal meaning of investing. Many people know the value of their IRA, 401-K or SEP retirement plans. But they aren't paying much attention to the investments that will last—namely, those they make in the next generation.

Our nation is crying out for more people who will mind the home, giving us a sense of stability and a future brimming with hope—hope that is found in enduring relationships, well-adjusted children and a personal relationship with Christ. My question is: Will you answer the call?

Questions for Reflection

1. Have you ever been in a situation where someone was supposed to watch out for your well-being and failed to carry through? How did that make you feel?
2. Have you ever had a friend whose marriage fell apart? Did you do anything to warn him or her about potential problems? Is there anything you could have done differently?
3. How do you feel when someone points out shortcomings in your life? Are you open to correction? Explain your answer.
4. When is the last time you spent at least a weekend alone with your spouse? If you can't remember, name three specific steps you can take to make that a reality.

5. Do you face temptations when you're away from home?
   How do you handle them? How do others hold you accountable when you return?
6. What steps are you taking to disciple your children? Another young person or a peer?

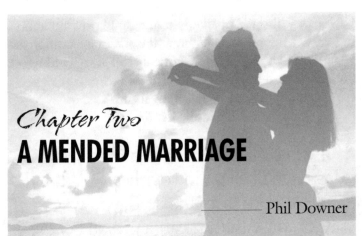

Chapter Two
A MENDED MARRIAGE

——— Phil Downer

Would you refuse a free gift? A death row inmate did. Convicted of robbing a United States mail carrier in 1829 in Pennsylvania, a prisoner named George Wilson awaited execution. Although an accomplice to the crime was executed, Wilson's life was spared when influential friends pleaded for mercy to President Andrew Jackson. The president offered him a pardon. Coming from the highest office of government, this is the most effective release from punishment.

However, there is a key distinction between pardon and exoneration. A pardon doesn't find the person innocent; it just covers his or her guilt. The law sees the purity of the pardon instead of that of the guilty party. So the individual first must admit guilt.

This is what the infamous Watergate defendants had to do in the 1970s. To gain a pardon, they first had to admit their guilt. That called for humility and brokenness. Yet it doesn't seem that difficult when the alternative is to spend more time behind bars or face the executioner. Accepting such a reprieve sounds reasonable to me.

Not to Wilson. Apparently bitter, stubborn and angry, he refused the pardon. It threw the state into an uproar. What should it do? The government offered to set him free but he spurned the overture.

"Execute him," the prosecution argued.

"No," replied the defense. "Let him go."

> "If you confess with your mouth Jesus as Lord, and believe in your heart that God raised Him from the dead, you will be saved; for with the heart a person believes, resulting in righteousness, and with the mouth he confesses, resulting in salvation."
> —Romans 10:9-10

The appeal reached the highest court in the land. *U.S. v. Wilson* appears in the law books as a striking commentary on the concepts of justice, mercy and unforgiveness. Famed Supreme Court Chief Justice John Marshall wrote the majority opinion. The court ruled that a pardon is "an act of grace." It is not a finding of innocence but a gift. You must receive it. The law recognizes the supremacy of the pardon over the actions of the individual. The pardon is perfectly legitimate and has full authority and effect if received.

However, because Wilson refused to receive it, he was still guilty. The highest court in the land affirmed the prosecution's argument—because Wilson refused the pardon, the verdict of guilt stood. He marched to his execution, having only to say the word to gain his freedom.

We could chalk this up to the ultimate in hardheadedness. But every day people enter eternity having refused the gift that could have gained them entrance into heaven. We are guilty of breaking God's law, yet He offers us a way out. Through believing in the sacrifice Christ made on the cross, we can secure an eternal pardon.

If you haven't taken this step yet, it is the first you need to make in order to guide your children properly. This book concerns how your marriage can make an eternal impact on your children. This is a demanding, challenging, serious responsibility, even if you do know Christ as Savior. Without Him you are headed for disaster. How do I know? Because that is the very road my wife, Susy, and I were traveling on when God rescued us.

A Walking Time Bomb

Can you imagine living with dents in the kitchen wall and knuckle marks on the dashboard of your car? Not to mention a snarling, enraged spouse who inflicted such damage by smashing telephone receivers and fists into the nearest object? That spouse was me. I was a walking time bomb, ready to explode at the least provocation.

Meanwhile, Susy wanted to divorce me. Only two things restrained her. One, she knew I really loved her. Two, divorce would be an admission she had made a mistake by marrying me. Great pride doesn't easily bend.

I didn't become a bundled mess of sharp-edged nerves overnight. It took years of practice. I started with slovenly attitudes toward work and school. That resulted in a one-way ticket out of the college where my father had been student body president. After flunking out of school at nineteen, I joined the U.S. Marine Corps. Soon they had trained me as an infantry machine gunner. I thought I was cool and tough.

After basic training and other preparation, I shipped out for South Vietnam. There I joined the Second Battalion in the northern part of the war-torn nation. It only took three weeks to learn a basic fact: The movies lied. The war films of John Wayne and Audie Murphy may have excited millions, but that wasn't reality.

War offers no glamour or heart-pounding exhilaration. Terror is a better word. It is horrible, the worst thing I could ever imagine. It remains the most awful experience of my life. In my outfit, killing and dying were routine. But something happened in Vietnam that would make an indelible impression on me.

> It didn't take much combat action
> to help me see a basic fact of life.
> The movies were fiction. In real life,
> war was horrible. It was an ugly,
> brutal, demanding, terrifying struggle
> to the death. It really was hell.

After I had been there for several months, my company led a helicopter assault into Antenna Valley. An enemy stronghold, it was a no-man's land for Americans. As we charged across the tarmac and loaded into the choppers, we had a sense of destiny. Some of us weren't coming back in one piece.

With the sun rising brightly across the mountains overlooking the valley, we zoomed over the horizon and into its mouth. After hitting the deck, we charged across an open rice paddy, ready to assault the enemy in the tree line: A surprise attack. But the surprise was on us.

The Vietcong had dug in with automatic weapons. They gunned us down like clay pigeons. In the first sixty to ninety seconds about a quarter to a third of our men were wounded or killed. Frantically we called for air strikes and artillery. Shells came screaming overhead, followed by F-4s. The planes hurtled by so low we could see the pilots in the cockpits. A concussion of bombs rattled our ears and shook the ground. But the enemy didn't withdraw. The flurry knocked out their supply lines and pinned them against us. Heavy fighting continued into the afternoon.

About mid-afternoon, the captain ordered my platoon to circle the left flank and relieve some pressure off our front. By that time, I had become the leader of a four-man machine gun team. Promotions had first moved me up from second ammo humper (the guy who carries the bullets), to first (the guy who feeds the bullets), to gunner. Right before this operation, I had been promoted to team leader. I led my team across the left flank, with the machine gun carried by one of my best friends, John Atkinson, who had been moved up by promotion to be the machine gunner.

Hitting an open area, we made a left-hand turn at a trail. John followed behind with the M-60 machine gun. Just as he made the turn, an enemy sniper opened up with an AK-47. As I dove toward the ground, a bullet went through the bottom of my pack and came out the top. It didn't hit me, but it broke my C rations and extra glasses. Next, a weight fell on me. John! With the exception of the bullet that pierced my pack, the rest of that volley had gone through my friend. I grabbed for his throat to see if I could find a pulse. Nothing. He was dead in my arms.

I felt like someone had reached into my insides and ripped my stomach out. Time froze. I thought of how my best buddy wouldn't be going home to the woman who had become his wife only months before he departed for Vietnam. Of the letter he had just received telling of her pregnancy. How he would never hear the word "daddy." But what really struck me as I lay there, pinned down by enemy fire, was that John had died in my place. The snipers had been aiming for the machine gunner. Three days earlier that would have been me.

Somehow I survived that attack. The enemy eventually withdrew, and I spent many more months fighting in Vietnam. I walked away while tens of thousands didn't. To this day, I sense the reason I'm alive is because others sacrificed themselves for me.

Know the feeling?

You may not have been through combat. But it is likely your parents struggled to give you a good life and make sure you had an education. Maybe a teacher inspired you to greatness. Whoever it was, you owe someone a debt of gratitude. When I returned from Vietnam, I would meet the One to whom I owe it all. But not before I endured more heartache.

A New Beginning

I may have had an admirable service record, but after Vietnam my former school history impressed no one. I still remember the admissions officer who looked over my résumé, references and kind letters written by my family and friends. When he got to my grades, he grimaced and whispered, "Oh." He asked why I had flunked college algebra—twice. I tried explaining how it was an 8 o'clock class and I had just never managed to make it.

"Well," he said, "we can't let you in here."

I finally found a junior college willing to give me a chance. Making the most of the opportunity, I worked hard and gained admission to Southern Methodist University. I'll never forget that first-year economics class where I met Susy. Having arrived a few minutes early, I was waiting for the professor to begin when she walked in. Wow! Dressed in a dark pantsuit, this beautiful, poised, confident young woman immediately caught my eye. I wondered, *What kind of a man would it take to marry a woman like that?*

> When I met Susy, my definition of a long-term relationship was, "Give me your phone number and maybe I'll call you next week." I thought I had to make up for all that lost time in Vietnam.

Until then I had approached post-military life with the idea that I needed to make up for lost time. I was dating a number of women and doing things I'm not proud to admit. For me a long-term relationship was, "Let me have your phone number and maybe I'll call you next week." But Susy changed all that. She swept me off my feet. When I learned she didn't smoke, I instantly quit a two-pack-a-day habit. We fell in love so deeply we couldn't wait to graduate from college before marrying. Later we enrolled in Emory Law School and moved on to high-paying, promising jobs.

While she went to work for Delta Air Lines in its law department, I joined a small law firm, sensing it was going places. Time proved me right and its staff quickly grew to fifty attorneys. What an opportunity! We were living the American dream.

Except for one thing. I learned again that Hollywood had lied. All those movies portrayed success, money, reputation and position as bringing peace and joy. Where was mine? I spent ten years lining up goals, knocking them down and still feeling miserable.

Emptiness gnawed at my insides. Not all the time, mind you. For a day or two, the latest bonus felt good. Winning cases or handsome financial settlements was always enjoyable. But that didn't relieve the pressure that stalked me like a hungry bear. Meanwhile our friends, social contacts and law partners grinned, "Look at that fine young couple."

In truth our marriage hung by threads. Behind closed doors we struggled with never-ending strife, frustration and anger. Especially anger. Rarely did I go through a day without blowing up at Susy. She always wanted to do the opposite of what I wanted to do. Living with a woman was difficult, especially since I was so self-centered.

Nor was work all that easy. I couldn't get along with the people, and the pressure of going to court reminded me of Vietnam: Though fought with cleaner uniforms and no physical contact, it still meant vicious combat.

Grasping at straws, we even joined a church. Over time I became an elder and Sunday school teacher. But I didn't find any peace in church work; I just found more work. (That isn't a negative statement about church, but about my outlook at the time.) Now I had another reason to blow my top, kick the cat and vent frustration.

When smashing the phone against the kitchen wall wasn't enough, I broke furniture and kicked walls. Something had to give: me.

The end of my old self came after I attended a meeting sponsored by Christian Business Men's Committee (CBMC).

I had never heard of CBMC, and I wasn't into attending religious events, but this was a businessmen's meeting. The speaker was Paul Johnson, a contractor from Detroit. He had a long list of credentials which intrigued me. Still, the main attraction was his occupation. I was preparing a case against a contractor, so I went to the luncheon hoping to get some tips on how to sue a contractor.

> "Woe to you, scribes and Pharisees, hypocrites! For you are like whitewashed tombs which on the outside appear beautiful, but inside they are full of dead men's bones and all uncleanness. So you, too, outwardly appear righteous to men, but inwardly you are full of hypocrisy and lawlessness."
> —Matthew 23:27-28

That day I hung on every word the speaker uttered, but not for the reason I expected. He talked about life the way it really was—the truth of our existence and the struggles he faced. He also discussed how his faith helped him meet those challenges. I had never heard a businessman talking about Jesus and what the Lord meant to his life.

My eyes opened wide when he said that I could know peace and joy right that moment by receiving Jesus Christ as Lord and Savior. He explained how Christ had walked this earth as all God and all man, that He had been crucified, died and was resurrected and that He had paid the penalty for me.

For the first time, I sensed how much God loved me. I began to get an understanding of what this funny gospel was all about.

Several weeks later I attended a retreat where other businessmen talked about the same thing. As I soaked up the discussions, I realized how Jesus Christ had taken my bullets. Long before John died in my arms, Jesus hung on the cross. A sinless, perfect Man died in my place to pardon my sin. I was still guilty, but God saw the purity of the pardon.

> My life changed dramatically. I found a peace, joy and contentment that I had never known existed. I knew God loved me—not because I was good, but just because I accepted His pardon.

It boiled down to the same decision that prisoner in Pennsylvania faced. When the free gift of salvation came into my life, the pardon covered my sin. All I had to do was accept the pardon. The night I reached that decision, I got down on my knees and embraced Christ. I confessed all that I had done wrong and my desperate need for Him.

My life changed dramatically. I found a peace, joy and contentment that I had never known existed. I knew God loved me—not because I was good, but just because I accepted his pardon. It overwhelmed me. My professional life became a mission instead of a burden. Finally I was able to love Susy in the way I had always wanted. But rather than describe it, I'll let her tell the story from her point of view.

Susy's Story

Susy Downer

I grew up in the Midwest in a warm, loving family. Active in church, we never even thought of being anywhere else on a Sunday. But something happened when I was fifteen months old that helped shape my character.

I contracted eczema, a skin disease that looks worse than poison ivy and itches continually. I lost all my hair and had to wear mittens to keep me from tearing my skin. I couldn't play outside because perspiration made me itch more. I didn't sleep through the night until I was four. Night after night, Mom talked to me to keep my mind off my itching.

While this may sound like a calamity, in reality it made me grow up—fast. Mom's nighttime conversations helped me mature rapidly. So did the avid reading I did in my time alone. I became so self-confident that when a mother instinctively pulled her child away in an elevator, I said, "Don't worry. It's just eczema and it's not contagious."

Because my parents perceived me as unusually responsible, they let me make major decisions. At the age of twelve, I started a swimming program in our backyard pool that grew from four students to seventy by the end of high school.

The summer after my freshman year of high school I decided I wanted to be a lawyer. Though female vocational aptitude wasn't fashionable then, I never deviated from that goal. Every day confirmed my belief that I was in total control of my life. My plans included graduating from college and law school before I would marry.

Then I met Phil. When we fell in love, I rationalized my previous time schedule. He seemed like the perfect man. Funny and relaxed, he loved me with all his heart. He loved to discuss weighty issues. He didn't think it ridiculous that I wanted to go to law school, like most other men I had dated.

We married in 1971 after our junior year of college and decided to take a semester off to go camping in Europe. What could be more romantic than spending four months in Europe without a care in the world? It was perfect.

> Secretly I made a deadline in my mind. If things didn't get better by a certain date, our marriage was over. The fights kept going. Yet I always found some reason, some little glimmer of hope, to push that date back.

That is, until the second day. When Phil misplaced something, it sent him into a rage. He screamed and yelled. I tried reasoning with him, but finally burst into tears. I cried myself to sleep that night. No one had ever yelled at me before. I wondered, *Who is this man that I've married?*

A pattern developed. Trifling irritations would trigger Phil's temper. He would yell and storm around, blaming me for whatever upset him. I would talk and reason with him but eventually would cry. My tears seemed to trigger his calming down. He would profusely apologize and promise never to do it again. But he seldom went more than a few days without a blowup.

These confrontations left me physically and emotionally exhausted. The only thing that kept me going was his penitent attitude. But as the days of arguments turned into weeks and the weeks into months, my love for Phil began slowly slipping away. Secretly I made a deadline in my mind that if things didn't improve by a certain date, it was over.

Not that all the times were bad. We had some enjoyable experiences that eased the pressure as we entered law school. We especially loved going to class and studying for exams together. We even argued as moot court partners. One time we had a legal brief due at 8 a.m. the next morning and had to stay up all night to finish it.

Just before dawn, I told Phil I was sleepy and had to go to bed for an hour. He told me I couldn't because we wouldn't finish in time. I went to bed anyway. After an hour, he awakened me and we started in again, Phil dictating while I typed. As the clock neared the magic hour, I realized we weren't going to finish. I started telling him how sorry I was when I noticed a twinkle in his eye.

"What is it?"

"Well, I just let you sleep for a minute and moved all the clocks forward an hour before I awakened you."

I was so grateful to have that extra hour that I couldn't get upset with him!

Despite the fights, there were enough of those good times to keep extending that deadline. Eventually I reasoned that once we graduated from law school, Phil would relax.

Then, about three years into our marriage, I met a woman named Liane at a baby shower who exhibited an unusual peace. Despite some incredibly harsh circumstances in her life, she told me God could handle any problem. At first that sounded inviting, but it didn't take long for me to reject the idea. Nobody could handle my life better than I could. Including God.

I thought my job at Delta in corporate law, securities and personnel work would be the answer to my problems. I loved the exciting, fulfilling work. Phil had landed a position with a growing firm; we were both grateful to be working after so many years of school. Yet in spite of the so-called security, a new home and the ability to travel just about anywhere thanks to my employer, our fights continued—all with the same pattern that had developed early in our marriage: Phil's yelling, my tears, our discussion and his promise never to do it again.

> Ever think a job promotion, big raise or the "perfect" vacation would bring you joy? I would have traded all the money, our home in the suburbs and free airline tickets for a little peace in our marriage.

How long could it continue? How many times could I push back my self-imposed deadline? Fortunately I never found out. Thanks to a Bible study called Operation Timothy that I eventually began doing with Liane, that woman I had met at the baby shower, and a women's retreat I attended soon after, life changed. On that retreat I realized for the first time that it was possible to have a personal relationship with Jesus Christ. Woman after woman talked about an alive and loving God who wanted to have that kind of relationship with me.

As I considered their claims, I faced the fact that I wasn't a Christian. I may have grown up in church and still attended services (half-heartedly), but I had never accepted Christ. I wasn't willing to give up my sacred independence—further evidence of my pride. As strange as it sounds, I knew this was what Phil needed, though.

I'll never forget when he had recently been to that CBMC meeting and heard about the claims of Christ and then went on the retreat where he accepted Him as Savior and Lord. We had a great week with no fights and the following Sunday we went to church. After coming home, I made dinner and we sat down to eat in front of the television. That was a habit from law school days, when study breaks consisted of dinner with the evening news. The only problem was that Phil had smashed all but one of our TV tables with his fist.

> God answers prayer. Nothing made that more real to me than the rekindled love He gave me for my husband. I didn't think I could spend the rest of my life with someone I didn't love. But Phil changed right before my eyes. It was marvelous!

That afternoon I must have said something that triggered his temper. I saw that familiar look of rage cross his face. As he raised his fist over that last, "quivering" TV table, a familiar feeling returned. I thought sarcastically, *Well, this changed life really lasted a long time.*

Suddenly Phil stopped, with his fist in midair, and said, "I'm going to go into the bedroom and pray. And I'm going to come back happy." When he did, the miracle overwhelmed me. A verse I had memorized with Liane immediately came to mind: "Therefore, if anyone is in Christ, he is a new creation; the old has gone, the new has come!" (2 Corinthians 5:17, NIV).

As Liane continued to disciple me, as I watched Phil gradually get a grip on his temper and as I continued to study the Bible and fellowship with other committed Christians, I realized how much God loved me. I finally admitted that whatever plan He had for my life would be better than anything I could plan myself.

Finally I said a simple prayer, telling God I understood my pride and independence were my great sins. Confessing that, I told him I wanted to change and go His way instead of my own.

For the first time, I knew the reality of the Lord Jesus living in me. I found a new peace and direction, one that has remained with me to this day.

Going Home

Now that Phil and I were both Christians, we lived happily ever after, right? Only in Hollywood! I realized that all those years of battle had just about killed the love I once felt for him. I knew it was wrong to leave but I just didn't think I could spend my whole life with someone I didn't love. But Liane had taught me well and I began to pray. I told the Lord, "You can do anything. Please, make me fall in love with Phil again."

God is so good. He answered that prayer completely. As Phil and I prayed together and grew in our newfound faith, I developed a love for him. It far surpassed the superficial feelings that led me to marry him, because this love was a direct gift from God. I marveled at how he grew sweeter and more loving each day. I say this confidently: If the Lord could save our marriage, there is no marriage beyond His healing touch.

Five more years passed before we had our first daughter, Abigail. During those first ten years of marriage, our careers took priority. Often we doubted we would ever have children. But as we watched the joy children brought to other Christian families, we wanted that too. When Abigail came into our lives, I couldn't believe how much I enjoyed motherhood. I didn't quit working, though. I loved my job too.

Two years later Paul was born. Still I continued working. We had a housekeeper we loved who made it possible to juggle responsibilities. I got up in the morning, read to the children and came back at noon for lunch to nurse the baby and read to Abigail. I was doing it all! But things changed dramatically when Abigail passed thirty months of age.

Suddenly she asked so many questions it felt like facing a verbal shotgun. As much as I loved our housekeeper, I realized she was answering those questions. She wouldn't necessarily answer them the same way I would. Conflict reigned. I loved my job so much I often said I would do it for free. But how could I ignore my responsibilities at home? Two young lives were rapidly maturing and I needed to mold and shape them.

Finally I mustered up enough courage to say a feeble prayer that God would make me want to do what He wanted me to do. It was the best I could manage. Over that next year He gradually changed my heart. Later I found the verse that explains the work the Lord did in my life. Philippians 2:13 (TLB) says, "For God is at work within you, helping you want to obey him, and then helping you do what he wants."

Other examples helped me too. I saw women who had given up rewarding jobs that they loved to invest themselves in their children. I caught the vision that children have eternal significance. Phil and I developed a burning desire to have as great an impact on the world as possible. And through this struggle we realized our impact would be multiplied if we imparted a vision for discipleship to our children.

This didn't happen overnight. But after years of staying home to raise our children and homeschool them, I know the joys and rewards. The task of building character and values into them has been a great challenge. By comparison, trying court cases for Delta Air Lines seems unimportant. Instead of affecting a corporation's bottom line, I am impacting the world for eternity. What a joy! How fulfilling! It is something no mother (or father) should miss.

Questions for Reflection

1. If you were convicted of a crime and sent to prison, what would you say if the governor offered to pardon you? Would you accept his gift if it meant admitting guilt?
2. How would you characterize your marriage? In what areas can you make it better?
3. Who sacrificed so that you could move ahead in life? How does that make you feel?
4. How are you investing in the younger generation?
5. Have you accepted Christ as your Lord and Savior? If not, what is keeping you from accepting this gift?
6. Do you have friends or loved ones who don't know Jesus? Are you willing to provide them the opportunity to turn their lives over to Christ?

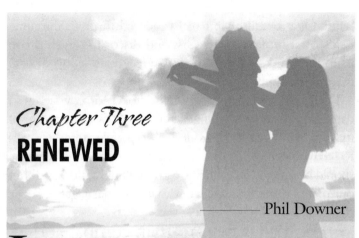

Chapter Three
RENEWED

—————— Phil Downer

I had just walked in the front door after several days on the road. This latest round of travel accentuated my hectic schedule. Times like these made it a struggle to balance my responsibilities as a father and husband with the demands of work. Boy, was I looking forward to a weekend of relaxation! Maybe I would catch a playoff game on the tube and take the kids to the park.

"Phil," my wife greeted me casually, "how are you doing?"

"Great," I smiled. "First weekend we've had off in a while."

What was that funny look in Susy's eyes?

"I'd really like you to paint our bedroom."

Paint the bedroom? I fumed to myself. *You've got to be out of your mind!*

I stood silently. The awful nature of the request sunk into my worn consciousness.

"So I'm supposed to paint *your* bedroom, huh?" I asked, twisting "your" into a long, sharp-edged verbal blade.

"It's *our* bedroom," she frowned back.

We resolved that situation without touching off World War III. That wouldn't have been possible early in our mar-

riage. Only because we have wandered through the mine
fields of arguments, bitterness and discord—which drove
us to the brink of divorce—do we feel qualified to discuss
marital harmony.

I believe one of the primary causes for divorce, which is so
damaging to today's younger generation, is the practice of
making marriage a battleground. Two people exert their wills
to see who comes out on top. The exact opposite is what we
should be doing. Only when we give willingly and care about
our mate's needs first will we reap happy marriages.

> Football is man-to-man combat and
> great fun for guys. But when it
> comes to marriage, this sport makes
> for a rotten outlook. Living with
> your mate is not a contact sport.

Men are especially guilty of not understanding this dynamic. As I travel across America, I see multitudes of men
who fail to see that marriage is not a football game. Don't
get me wrong: I love football. Even though we live in Tennessee, I spent time in Texas and developed a long-lasting
love for the Dallas Cowboys.

I'll never forget my youthful days on the playing field, striving to win all the marbles. Even guys who never dreamed of
suiting up for the varsity can relate to my story. In nearly every young boy lives the heart of a would-be football hero.

But men, it's time to give up those boyhood memories.
When it comes to living happily ever after, we must shuck
the gridiron mentality. Marriage is not a contact sport. It is
the exact opposite. Instead of trying to prove who's best,

partners already know the answer: their mate. They love the other person so much they can't wait to serve her (or him) and help their spouse to reach her goals. Teamwork replaces competition.

If men retain a "hit 'em again, harder, harder" outlook, they will spend life rushing by the people they profess to love the most. Acting like the king of the hill, they strive to conquer new challenges while barely stopping to say hello. They will brush by their children as if they're strangers (and in many cases they are). They will treat their wives like hired servants.

> After three decades of marriage, it is still easy for Susy and I to disagree. On some things, we just don't see eye-to-eye and probably never will. We had to learn to appreciate our differences and work together in order for our marriage to endure.

Even worse is treating your spouse like an expendable bystander. I still remember the time in our battling days when I was in the middle of an argument with Susy. Boy, I was on a roll! She had let me down and made all these mistakes. I confidently rattled through the list with all the poise and debating skills I had learned in law school.

Suddenly the phone rang. Right in the middle of another "I can't believe you did so and so and so" statement, I picked up the receiver, calmly said, "Hello," and chatted amiably with a supervisor from work. "Of course, absolutely," I said in my most persuasive, you-can-count-on-me voice. "No problem at all. I can take that on. Good-bye."

As soon as I hung up, I jumped full steam back into the argument. Sound familiar?

One key to resolving tension with your mate is understanding—and appreciating—your differences. Susy and I have been married for three decades. We graduated from the same university. After marrying and getting our bachelor's degrees, we went to the same law school and sat side by side in nearly every class, taking all the same courses except one.

After law school, we put our education to work and made a great living. We both tried cases in the courtroom. Later we admitted our personal lives were out of control and accepted Jesus as Savior the same year. We went to the same churches, heard the same messages and attended the same conferences.

Yet despite all these years together, when she goes left, I insist on turning right. She craves strawberry; I like chocolate. She orders thin crust; I, deep dish. She is always ready to invite enough friends over to fill the house and the backyard. I want to collapse on the couch and enjoy peace and quiet. We are two very different people.

Transformed Thinking

With the Christian divorce rate surpassing the world's,[1] something is wrong. We need to transform our thinking, starting with overcoming the past. Unless we resolve underlying problems, old wounds will fester. The pain will prevent us from walking in the fullness of a good relationship with Christ—and our mate.

Before coming to Christ, I exhibited the classic symptoms of a cup full of pain. Escape from reality, addictions, compulsive behavior, burnout, sleep disturbances, depression, controlling behavior, impatience and a critical spirit are among the many symptoms. Besides damaging an individual's life, such behavior doesn't create a happy home, either.

Personal renewal is wonderful, but if it doesn't carry over into your marriage and family relationships, any claims of transformation will ring hollow to those closest to you. This is why as a Christian I had to start mending my relationship with Susy. Thanks to my thoughtlessness and old habits, I had nearly ruined it.

In the last chapter Susy talked about how I blew up at her on the second day of our honeymoon in Europe. Was it because I had misplaced something and blamed it on her? Was I that upset over such a trivial thing? No. I had just walked through a mountain of pressure. A new family, in-laws, a church full of people, seeing my Vietnam buddies and the memories that stirred up . . . it combined to create a monumental personal challenge.

To show you how nervous I was, despite often partaking of the world's pleasures then, I didn't throw a bachelor party the night before my wedding. The night I pledged to be pure to my wife a ton of emotions welled up inside of me. Add to that the hassles of overseas travel and my cup was ready to spill over—abundantly. Naturally I exploded all over the person closest to me.

After accepting Christ I found a new way. He can drain the pain, cover our guilt, forgive us and help us walk in newness of life. Yet the old ruts carved by our body, past thinking, unresolved emotions and the old human will must be smoothed over by the renewing of our mind.

This sounds a bit contradictory. After all, didn't we previously quote Second Corinthians 5:17, which says a man in Christ is a new creation? This is true, but we also have to *grow* as a new creation, which is a lifelong process.

After all, if your cup is full of stress, shame, guilt, fear, insecurity, resentment, pain and disappointment, it won't get emptied overnight. It takes time to let go of those negative emotions and replace them with love. I had to work to shed my stress, fatigue, guilt and anxiety.

Of course, mending my relationship with Susy was only the beginning. As the years go by, I must continually confess my faults and repair any damage I inflict not only on Susy but on our children as well. This calls for honesty, humility and openness. Being transparent is not just important for building relationships in the home. It will also help your children be transparent with you instead of hiding their problems and winding up in even worse disasters.

I remember the time I walked downstairs, obviously upset. I told my family, "OK, everybody around the table. We're going to talk." After everyone settled into a chair, I confessed, "I'm really struggling with something."

I watched as six pairs of little eyes grew big, wondering why I was so mad. "I am really having trouble forgiving this man," I continued, explaining I had had a disagreement with someone on my staff.

"You know, I have taught you guys two possibilities about a person who can't forgive. I want you to tell me what they are. What are they?"

They all sat silently, looking as if they were afraid to respond. Finally our oldest son, Paul, said, "Well, the first thing is, maybe the person is not a Christian."

His brothers and sisters looked at him like he had lost his mind. How dare he say that?

"Well, I think I'm a Christian," I said. "What's the other reason?"

"Well, the other reason is that the person is in sin," he replied.

"That's not what I wanted to hear, but I think that's the truth," I said. I had to confess that by not forgiving this man I was in the wrong. From hearing my children talk about it later, I know this made a significant impact on them. Being willing to humble myself and be honest about my weakness let them know they didn't have to be perfect either.

None of us has an easy time forgiving. Even easygoing, understanding people occasionally hit brick walls. But that day our children learned that forgiving others is the right thing to do. So is taking such sticky issues to prayer. As we sat around the table, I asked, "Would you pray for me?" They responded in unison and we all drew closer.

> "Then Peter came and said to Him, 'Lord, how often shall my brother sin against me and I forgive him? Up to seven times?' Jesus said to him, 'I do not say to you, up to seven times, but up to seventy times seven.' "
> —Matthew 18:21-22

Far too many parents think that if they admit to weakness, their children won't respect them. That is simply not true. Teenagers in particular resent parents who try to pretend they're perfect and never admit they make a mistake.

If parents confess their struggles, so will their children. Our oldest daughter, Abigail, has often come to us when she is wrestling with a problem or difficult decision. Because we set the pattern, she doesn't hesitate to say, "I'm really struggling with this. Would you help me? Would you pray for me and keep me accountable to work in this area?"

Family is the one place where everyone should feel comfortable about expressing doubts and finding support and solace. By sharing only your strengths you build walls. By sharing weaknesses you build bridges. Rather than being a disgrace, this helps create stronger relationships. Powerful relationships with God and your family will enhance your ability to minister to those around you.

I call it the "love cup." Our goal for building relationships is to strengthen ourselves and those we love with peace, joy and hope. We want to walk around like a cup full of Christ. Bump us and instead of cracking up with anger and resentment, we spill out understanding and reconciliation.

Accountability

Along the way I need people to hold me accountable for my actions. Because of our innate blind spots, we can think we're doing just fine but overlook that we've offended others or let them down. One of the natural places to find this accountability for our actions, treatment of people and faithfulness in our Christian life is right at home. Especially with our mate. Who knows us better and can discern our motives?

The bottom line is this: We can fool a lot of people with our "public" face, but that doesn't wash so easily at home. Our human inclination is to avoid accountability because we don't like being challenged or prodded.

As I matured in my spiritual walk and thought about life's ultimate goal, I realized it didn't come down to the model of car I drove, the size of my house or my bank balance. When I dug deep enough, I recognized that I wanted to be like Christ. Face it—that's a pretty tall order. Christ? Me? How is that ever going to happen?

This is why transforming ourselves and renewing our lives is such a painstaking, time-consuming process. It will always be something we are moving toward. If I get serious, it doesn't take long to fill up ten fingers, listing areas where I need to improve. I need help in this process. This is why God gave us a spouse. As we draw closer in an intimate relationship, we see the things that keep us from melding into one spirit in the bond of true friendship.

> "We also exult in our tribulations, knowing that tribulation brings about perseverance; and perseverance, proven character; and proven character, hope; and hope does not disappoint, because the love of God has been poured out within our hearts through the Holy Spirit who was given to us."
> —Romans 5:3-5

As issues come to light, we can deal with them. This is the purpose of accountability, where two people get below the surface and delve into what really matters. David and Jonathan are excellent examples of this. First Samuel 18:1-4 outlines their deep friendship. Verse 1 says, "The soul of Jonathan was knit to the soul of David, and Jonathan loved him as himself."

This illustrates the first point of accountability:

1. *Commitment.* Without commitment you will burn out along the way. An accountable relationship will bring great joy, but it also will irritate and upset you. Our human de-

sire is to have everyone pat us on the back, not challenge us. But when we get really personal and dig down deep, we may not like what we find.

The joy that comes from a deep relationship will be much more than whatever pain it took to sew it together as the Lord intended it. A covenant is a serious relationship where two people become one. Marriage is a covenant so serious that God told His children not to tear it apart.

If you read on to First Samuel 18:4, you see that "Jonathan stripped himself of the robe that was on him and gave it to David, with his armor." This illustrates the second and third points of accountability:

> ## "So they are no longer two, but one flesh. What therefore God has joined together, let no man separate." · —Matthew 19:6

2. Transparency. Two people can't form bonds when one wants to discuss personal issues and the other is hung up on soap operas—or football. As each person becomes transparent and shows his or her weaknesses, it allows God to start working between them. His Spirit does the work. We can't become like Christ through our own strength or our spouse's. We're too far from that goal. It happens as Christ works in us.

3. Vulnerability. When Jonathan gave his armor to David, he took down his protection and his wall. How often do you walk up to someone and in the first fifteen seconds you can see that the only significant thing you may learn about the person is his or her name? Initial contacts often don't run very deep. But in this relationship, Jonathan made himself vulnerable to David.

I don't necessarily embrace vulnerability with passion and enthusiasm. But I have formed this kind of accountability with Susy and our children. For example, I spend one-on-one time with Paul, which calls for rearranging our schedules and opening up to each other. We get up at a very early hour and sit at the table. We unload our anxieties, fears and plans for the day. We look at what Scripture has to say about these things.

> "And if one can overpower him who is alone, two can resist him. A cord of three strands is not quickly torn apart."
> —Ecclesiastes 4:12

We don't have much of an agenda. We're just honest and real with each other. God can work through that. We don't understand how He does that, but He honors our motives when we declare, "I'm going to be vulnerable and honest with this person and trust You with the rest." He has faithfully built our relationship through mutual vulnerability.

4. Sharing struggles. Verse 4 of Second Samuel 18 also says that Jonathan gave David his sword, bow and belt. Remember, in this time period there were wars going on everywhere you looked. Like Jonathan, David had become part of Saul's army. Here was the king's son, sharing the finest weaponry in Israel with his friend. They were likely encrusted with jewels and plated with gold. But giving away such goods wasn't important. They were friends and shared everything, including enemies.

Imagine the strength and energy David received from
the gift of Jonathan's belt, which some translations identify
as a girdle. This represented a man's abdominal strength.
Getting into close relationships takes a lot of strength and
energy—or, as my drill instructor would have put it,
"guts"—not to mention stamina and patience. When you
get close to someone, you won't always see a pretty picture.

The wise King Solomon wrote that a cord twined together with three strands is not easily broken. That is the
glory of such relationships. When two people are committed to forming a deep friendship and God is in the middle
of it, it is like a three-strand cord. You can make it work.

Naturally, for accountability to succeed, confidentiality
must be a foundational principle. Nobody is going to be
willing to uncover his deepest emotions unless he is convinced they will remain a secret. Trust violated is trust destroyed. Wives, when your husband reveals an intimate
detail of his life, that is not fodder for discussion in the coffee shop or a women's weekend retreat.

Growing in Grace

If you grew up in a Christian home, with stable influences and parents who are still married after thirty, forty or
fifty years together, you are blessed. But that doesn't mean
you don't need to pay attention to personal renewal. Parents, you must set the standard. As your children watch you
grow spiritually, they will realize conforming to God's image is a lifelong process.

After hearing my story of growing up in a chaotic home
environment and being exposed to the rough-and-tumble
of the marine corps, my children used to think they didn't
need a "quiet time." They figured that was something Dad

needed since he was the one with all the past problems to overcome. Wrong.

We live in a society full of bad attitudes, misguided teaching and media influences that sink progressively lower on the morality scale. Each of us must constantly fill our minds with the Bible instead of the junk streaming from movies, television, radio, magazines and books. It is a fight to remember what God thinks about issues when all around us are voices telling us to do the opposite.

I remember when our middle son, Matthew, grappled with the idea of meeting with the Lord every day. He bought a special devotional Bible, yet in spite of constant church attendance and Christian teaching in our home, he struggled to stick with it. He now admits his pride is the only thing that kept him going. He didn't want to admit he was a quitter.

However, when he was faithful to his daily commitments, he started enjoying it and then thriving on it. He would look forward to getting into God's Word, praying and spending time with the Lord and understanding His perspective on life. One of the verses that benefited his daily life came from Ephesians 4:29: "Let no unwholesome word proceed from your mouth, but only such a word as is good for edification according to the need of the moment, so that it will give grace to those who hear."

Matthew is pretty witty and always has a lot to say, but because of Scripture he saw that unless his speech would be uplifting he shouldn't say it. It helped him keep his mouth closed more often and led to less friction with his brothers and sisters.

Despite this growth, he needed encouragement to keep going. More than once I would ask, "Matthew, have you had your quiet time this morning?" and he would shake his head, "No." I gently reminded him of his need to spend time with

God. There is no way we can live like the Lord wants us to
live if we don't spend time with Him. Matthew didn't always
care for this prodding, but today he appreciates how wonderful it is to have someone keeping him accountable.

Personal growth is vital to family relationships as well. For
all the strong belief I have in family, the truth is it isn't always
easy maintaining a sense of calm and love at home. Eight different people with eight sets of ideas, opinions, tastes and desires are bound to clash. Without love and forgiveness, we
can't make it. Without getting into God's Word on a regular
basis, we can't make it.

As I mentioned before, hardly a month goes by that I don't
read about some famous ministry leader or Christian "per-
sonality" getting a divorce. Everyone is susceptible to problems, temptations and struggles. We can't neglect spiritual
growth and expect it to have no impact on our personal relationships. We don't want to ruin the very thing that we wish
to maintain.

Just as we need to stay in constant contact with God, we
need to pay close attention to our family. We can't treat our
loved ones casually, demonstrate a lack of commitment or
care, explode at them constantly and still expect to reap love
and rewards. We must show them how much we care by
spending time with them and building relationships of trust.

We also need to work to overcome past hurts we have inflicted on our mate or children. Like the time I was on a
date with our daughter Anna and told her about the fear I
had as a youngster because of my parents' never-ending arguments. I would go to bed and they were arguing; when I
woke up they were still at it (or so it seemed).

As I talked, I remembered the time Susy and I had argued and Anna heard us because her bedroom is at the head

of the stairs. Maybe she had suffered the same kind of fear. When she admitted she had, I apologized and asked her to forgive me. I told her I was wrong and that Susy and I had resolved the problem. That may sound like no big deal, but it was a major step forward that strengthened my relationship with Anna.

Fortunately Anna was prepared to discuss this issue at the time I brought it up. I believe the Lord was prompting me to discuss it when I did, which goes back to the value of my daily quiet time. If you feel a need to discuss (or confront) an issue with a family member or friend, be sure to pray about it first. If you ask the Lord for guidance, He will give it to you—and not just the right words, but even the right time.

One way I think the Lord does this is by softening the other person's heart. Sometimes when feelings have been injured, time needs to pass before reconciliation can occur. But when God touches the other person's heart, he or she will be willing to listen to what you have to say. The Lord may even bring that person to a realization of what you're thinking without your saying anything.

Susy had a close friend who often submitted her concerns about her husband to God. If she found a verse in the Bible that represented how she felt God wanted him to act, she marked it in her Bible and prayed that verse for him. Once her husband had come to her and shared with her that the Lord had shown him something about his life that wasn't right. He made a commitment to improve.

His wife got her Bible, opened to a verse on that point and showed him where she had been praying for him on that issue for the past year. Can you imagine how that strengthened their faith, and the husband's trust in his wife, that she was willing to wait on the Lord for her husband to change?

Galatians 5:22-23 outlines the fruit of the Holy Spirit: "love, joy, peace, patience, kindness, goodness, faithfulness, gentleness [and] self-control." When this kind of fruit is present in marriages and families, homes will be filled with joy. The old plagues of fear, anxiety and anger will fade away in the light of God's love.

Questions for Reflection

1. What kind of junk was present in your life in the past? What steps are you taking to make sure it stays in the past?
2. Who has been a positive influence in your spiritual life? Explain how this person has helped you.
3. How has your life been transformed by Christ? What changes do you still need to make (or allow Him to make)?
4. Describe an experience when you forgave someone for hurting you. What kind of change did that make in your life?
5. Does your mate hold you accountable for your actions? How do you incorporate all four aspects of accountability listed in this chapter? If you haven't, what steps do you need to take to do so?
6. How have you tried to build closer relationships within your family?

Note

1. George Barna, "Christians Are More Likely to Experience Divorce Than Are Non-Christians" [on-line], December 21, 1999. June 10, 2003. Available for purchase from: <http://www.barna.org/cgi-bin/PageProduct.asp?ProductID=66>.

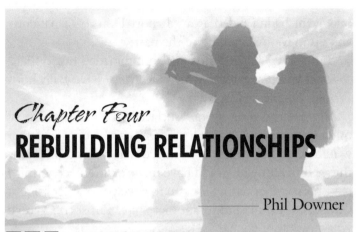

Chapter Four
REBUILDING RELATIONSHIPS

——— Phil Downer

W hat matters most in life is how we finish—not the past, the stupid mistakes we made, the pains we suffered or the horrendous childhood we endured. A friend I'll call Don saw that as he worked to mend his battered relationship with his son. Don came to Christ late in life. Of course, his concern then turned to his son, Brad. He knew he needed to ask his son's forgiveness for all the pain he had inflicted on him before he could expect his son to listen to the claims of Christ.

At age sixty, he took his thirty-year-old son for a weekend of fishing. But his heart wasn't on rods and reels. As they talked out on the lake, Don finally gathered enough courage to say, "I just want to confess to you that I was an alcoholic and I was unfaithful. I know the family you grew up in and all the things I did brought great pain to you."

Brad nodded. "That's right, Dad, it did."

Soon the younger man gushed forth a story of the pain and anguish a particular incident had caused him as a boy, revealing the damage his father's irresponsibility had inflicted on him and his mother. The humiliation of just that one event hadn't faded away. It hurt Don to sit patiently and listen to this retelling of the past.

"I'm sorry," he said after his son unloaded his feelings. "Would you please forgive me? That must have really hurt. Would you please forgive me?"

All weekend long stories surfaced as Brad thought of other episodes that had hurt him. When he did, his father would say, "You're right. I can see that if I had just done things differently, it would have made a difference. It must have been embarrassing for you to have your father gone at Christmas, drunk and in another state. I'm sorry. Would you please forgive me?"

> **"Then I will make up to you for the years that the swarming locust has eaten, the creeping locust, the stripping locust and the gnawing locust, My great army which I sent among you."**
> **—Joel 2:25**

Don humbled himself constantly throughout the trip. Finally Brad broke. Bursting into tears, he clutched his father and held tight. That day they began rebuilding the razor-thin threads of their relationship. Both Don and his son know the Lord today and are very close. They pray together, among other things asking that Brad's children will grow up to become servants of God. Don and his wife recently led one of their grandchildren to accept Christ as Savior. They are confident the rest will take that step too.

The Lord can retake ground and restore damaged relationships. It is impossible to restore the years gone by, but with God in your marriage and family, you can embrace a brighter future. As a friend once said, "The jury is out on all of us." We can't do anything about the past, but we have a lot to say about what happens in our lives from this day forward. There is still time to make an impact. There is still time to rebuild damaged relationships.

Trouble at Home

While alcoholism, drug abuse and other dysfunctional behavior affect millions of people, for millions more they aren't a major problem. It is the simple, day-to-day misunderstandings, disagreements and irritations of living with spouses or family members that cause serious breaks in their relationships. How we react to these situations and affirm our love for the person, despite our disagreements, makes all the difference in the world.

A few years ago our son Joshua went through a rough period. Whether you call it moodiness, adolescent rebellion or a bad hair day, he became a severe pain at home. He was disrespectful to Susy—talking back to her, disobeying her, being lazy or shooting her rotten looks when she asked him to do something. He acted in similar ways toward his brothers and sisters. Susy gave him some minor discipline, but not enough to get his attention.

Finally when Susy and I were out one night for dinner, she told me what had been happening. When we returned home, we gathered everyone together and confronted Joshua. We told him what he had done wrong and how it had hurt others. Opening the Bible to First Corinthians 13, I asked him to read the famous chapter on love.

When he finished, I asked, "Do you love your mom?"
"Yes."

"Is this the way you've been acting?"

"No," he shook his head.

His brothers and sisters shared how he had been rude and thoughtless toward them. Susy listed several ways in which he had shown disrespect or disobedience. He didn't try to defend himself, because he knew it was true. Everyone warned him he had to clean up his act. But he also needed discipline.

"Baseball's over," I said, demanding his glove and bat. Then I banished him from shooting at the goal hanging above the driveway and told him, "Basketball's over too. For the indefinite future, your free time is going to be filled up with chores and Scripture reading, plus writing down key verses. The kitchen is now yours too. Keep it clean after every meal and during the day. You can go up in your room and spiff it up. I'll be up there in a while."

> "An angry man stirs up strife,
> and a hot-tempered man
> abounds in transgression."
> —Proverbs 29:22

I took no pleasure in handing out that kind of punishment, but Joshua needed a severe course correction. He later talked about how this discipline made him realize that his conduct was wrong. It takes humility to admit mistakes, but that is the first step toward healing damaged relationships.

In our son's case, he realized that he had been taking out his anger on everyone else in the family. If someone did something that Joshua didn't like, he snapped at him. Anger is natural, but taking out your anger on others is wrong.

Scripture helped change his attitude. So did his early-morning sessions with God. He saw how a daily quiet time gave him a chance to tell the Lord about his burdens and to seek direction.

We also established an accountability time. Early in the morning we sometimes run a mile together or lift weights, which gives us a chance to talk things over. He asks me what is happening at the office and how Susy and I are getting along. I ask him how he's doing in school and if he is getting along with his brothers and sisters.

Joshua will quickly tell you that these sessions aren't always positive. Like discipline, accountability is not necessarily pleasant. Yet we need it to grow in our spiritual lives and relationships. Too many people treat correction as something they only have to do when an authority figure is close by. But the goal of an upright walk with God is to act properly even when nobody else is present.

Our whole family learned some valuable lessons from this incident. Everyone saw that confrontation can be handled in a Christlike manner. We set no time limit on this session so everyone could think things over and feel free to speak or to not say a word. We emphasized that love was the motive for this session, not anger. We wanted the outcome to fit with God's desires, so we prayed about it. We prayed that He would give His blessing for what we said and did.

As we began, Susy and I encouraged our children to think about something each of us could have done differently. Sure, Joshua was primarily at fault. But his siblings had taken actions to provoke him, incite his anger or discourage him by showing a lack of respect. When we had seen he was going through a hard time, we hadn't prayed enough for him. We encouraged Joshua to talk about his feelings too so he didn't feel like he was being steam-rollered.

Often when facing criticism, we can be quick to say, "I'm just a failure," and get very discouraged. So we went around in a circle. Everyone listed ways they could have acted differently and took responsibility for their actions. Each of us apologized for our mistakes.

We concluded with each person sharing something he or she appreciated about Joshua. We told him he has a wonderful spirit and how his enthusiasm and excitement is contagious. We explained how that encourages us.

> "This you know, my beloved brethren.
> But everyone must be quick to hear,
> slow to speak and slow to anger;
> for the anger of man does not
> achieve the righteousness of God."
> —James 1:19-20

This is the way we try to turn the necessary giving and receiving of criticism into an encouraging session where we can learn from our mistakes. Some families take charge of problems while others retreat. But the Bible admonishes us to deal with issues in love, truth and honesty. Granted, it isn't easy to find a balance with such matters, but this hard work pays off.

Life Application

One thought that crossed my mind when Joshua was going through his six-week punishment was, *I can't imagine that*

I could do as well with that. Growing up, I never knew how to handle correction. Because of the circumstances in our home, I developed two reactions to confrontation—defense and vengeance.

In school when I was growing up people would pick on me. They'd laugh at my father, my mother or the ambulance in front of the house. You see, when I was about ten years old I came home from school to an eerily quiet house. I called to Mom several times, and after no answer, found her in a pool of blood after her first attempted suicide. Because of my parents' boisterous fighting, and my father's rather public philandering, we were already the talk of the neighborhood. But when my mother was taken by ambulance to the hospital and then to a local mental institution, my family became the butt of jokes and gossip to which I responded with my fists, attempting to defend my family and soothe my pain. Whoever thinks children can't be cruel lives in a dream world. Naturally I developed a short fuse. If anyone pushed me a tad, I pushed back harder. I would come home with blood all over my knuckles from the fights.

I carried this defensive attitude into marriage. I wanted to win, retain control, always be right, be appreciated and have it all my way. That may win a war but it doesn't build a relationship. It wasn't just at home, either. All my relationships were that way. Years later I am still working to overcome these tendencies.

This is why I am such a strong believer in Scripture. Take, for example, the lesson in the twelfth chapter of Hebrews, which includes one of the most powerful biblical passages in facing day-to-day struggles with anger, anxiety, frustration and criticism. These are the primary causes of many problems with marital and other interpersonal relationships. Any time I feel pain or something goes wrong I turn to this chapter in Hebrews. I want to know if God is trying to teach me something, if this is a form of discipline the Lord is taking me through.

For a real-life application, I remember the day I locked my keys inside my car just as a snowstorm was gathering. I couldn't call our office to tell employees to go home until I found help to get me out of this mess. My initial reaction was to fume about the circumstances. When I calmed down, I meekly asked, "God, what do You have in this for me? I want to grow and be like Christ."

> "Therefore, since we have so great a cloud of witnesses surrounding us, let us also lay aside every encumbrance and the sin which so easily entangles us, and let us run with endurance the race that is set before us, fixing our eyes on Jesus, the author and perfecter of faith, who for the joy set before Him endured the cross."
> —Hebrews 12:1-2

After further reflection, I had to admit my blame for causing the situation. I had focused on myself instead of others. That day I had been preoccupied with cashing in some frequent flier points to save money on a flight. Though supposedly for the organization, I still had a vested interest in this thrifty transaction. It would make me look good.

Meanwhile, everyone else had a wary eye trained on the severe weather forecast. But why would that bother me? I had always prided myself on withstanding any kind of storm. Back when I worked for a law firm based in Atlanta, I had hopped an early-bird flight to Washington, D.C., to open a new branch. The snow was flying, but I grabbed a cab to the office and cheerfully answered calls from lawyers in Virginia and Maryland saying they couldn't make it in because of the snow.

"The roads are fine," I had said. "We'll see you in about thirty minutes."

This sort of attitude stuck with me for years. So as I headed out the door and my secretary asked, "What are we going to do about the bad weather coming?" I responded, "What weather? You can never count on weathermen."

"Well, there is a big snowstorm coming," she repeated.

"Oh, it'll never stick. Don't worry about it."

My pride in pushing through storms drove my outlook that day—though not nearly as much as those frequent flyer tickets. Well, despite my statement as I walked out the office door, when I drove downtown, it started snowing. I tossed some money in the parking meter and turned around to walk inside the ticket office.

Suddenly I realized I had locked the car door behind me with the engine still running. I frantically called the office and got the numbers for my keys, which my secretary had in a file. Then I called a cab and had him run me to a dealership to get new keys made.

When I got back to my car, I sat there thinking, *This is so dumb. Why is this happening? Lord, what are You trying to teach me?* Like a breath of fresh air, my thoughts cleared. God showed me how selfish I had been. I was more concerned about my interests than an office full of people who needed to get home. I had to call my secretary again and confess, "I'm sorry I was looking after my interests and not yours. Send everybody home."

Then I went to the airline, proudly waving my coupons to cash in on this special offer. But the woman behind the counter said, "I'm sorry, our deal doesn't work with that kind of ticket." Talk about humiliating!

Just to round out the picture, after I told my secretary to send everyone home, I had added, "I still say it'll never stick." Right. Twenty-four inches of snow fell that day and we didn't have a shovel or kerosene lantern in the house when the power flickered off.

When something awkward happens in my life I try first to look at myself. Susy will tell you I'm not always faithful, but I try. When you run into similar irritations or circumstances in your workplace or home, avoid the human tendency to criticize, defend yourself or look for vengeance. Pray first and ask, "Lord, how have I blown it? Would You show me my sin? Was I prideful? Was I not looking out for someone else first?"

This will, as Hebrews 12:1 says, help us lay aside every sin and encumbrance. Sometimes we have sin in our lives; other times it's just a hindrance. Saving the ministry money on frequent flier points wasn't a sin. However, by keeping me from doing what I should have been doing, it represented an obstacle to taking the correct action.

Hebrews 12 also talks about fixing our eyes on Jesus. Doing that helps us realize what a severe penalty He paid on our behalf. If we can grasp what kind of pain He endured for us, it will help us deal with less earth-shattering circumstances in our own lives. It may also help us recognize when we are encountering the Lord's discipline, as I was that day.

"I'm Sorry"

Those are two of the simplest, yet most powerful words ever spoken when it comes to healing and rebuilding relationships. But what I've had to learn over the years is that a simple "I'm sorry" often doesn't cut it. Especially if I speak it with no conviction, casual body language and no pledge to change my behavior so I don't repeat the mistake.

Apologies should be more like, "Susy, I am *really sorry* that I was worried about my work. I wasn't tuned in to the Lord like I should have been and came home in a grumpy mood. My response over what went wrong with the kids was totally inappropriate. I was out of line. That must have really hurt. I could have handled that with a gentle word. I'll use this lesson to make changes."

> "MY SON, DO NOT REGARD LIGHTLY THE DISCIPLINE OF THE LORD, NOR FAINT WHEN YOU ARE REPROVED BY HIM; FOR THOSE WHOM THE LORD LOVES HE DISCIPLINES, AND HE SCOURGES EVERY SON WHOM HE RECEIVES."
> —Hebrews 12:5-6

Confession begins with repentance, followed by a sign of understanding how it felt. The worst thing men do is take their spouse for granted. Susy oversees cleaning, cooking and other household chores on top of homeschooling our children and helping in our ministry. If you think that's easy, try scrubbing a few toilets after dealing with children all day. There's a lot that goes on!

For me to walk in and immediately bark orders or fume about a perceived slight is like throwing a bucket of cold water on everyone. Whether we realize it or not, husbands are the spiritual leaders in our homes. We either lead upward or downward.

Apologies to your children may be in order as well. Not only will this improve their outlook, it will make you more sensitive. When I do this, it gives me a sense of how they feel. When I start to feel how they feel, it hurts. The next time a stressful situation arises, I may remember not to choose the flesh over the Lord.

> I face two temptations when confronted with the need to make amends or change. The first is to brush it off and treat it lightly. The second is to get discouraged.

It also shows remorse and models how I want our children to act. Everyone knows how often, as a child, you were selfish and needed to apologize for your actions. But if the parent isn't demonstrating how that is done, the child never learns to embrace humility.

I think one reason we hate saying "I'm sorry" is that it reminds us of failure and how much we disliked correction as a child. Yet Hebrews goes on to remind us that God disciplines His sons. If we're not under discipline, seeing God's correction in our life, we're not His children. I want to receive the Lord's correction as a son wants his father's guidance. If we strive to faithfully follow God and submit to His discipline, we will reap righteousness.

On one of our early morning runs, Paul said, "Dad, there's nothing like a clear conscience."

"That's right," I agreed. "Nothing like it."

If I can live openly with my family and in an honest relationship with the Lord, I can reap the sweet fruit of righteousness. One way to ensure I do that is to apologize when my actions warrant it. I don't think it will ever become easy. But I know the end result will bring the kind of love and strong bonds I want—not only in my home, but in my children's homes when they marry and have children.

Maintaining this kind of open, humble attitude will help me follow the Lord's instruction in Hebrews 12:12, to "strengthen the hands that are weak and the knees that are feeble." In other words, God is saying, "Stop pouting and grow up." Being an adult is no guarantee of maturity. I've seen people in their sixties and seventies act like spoiled five-year-olds when they don't get their own way.

Nor am I perfect when it comes to maturity. There are two things I struggle with. When God shows me something I've done wrong, or one of our children comes to me with a complaint, my first inclination is to brush it off. Big mistake! I should never treat the Lord's admonition or someone else's injury lightly.

My other temptation is to get discouraged. The devil jumps on my shoulder and whispers, "See what you did? You're no good. You're insufficient."

God doesn't want us to get discouraged. We're not perfect and He doesn't expect us to be. But He does want us to stand up, admit it if we made a mistake and go on. Too often I am inclined to wallow in self-pity. In reality this is upside-down pride. When I moan, "I'm terrible," it's because I want others to pat me on the back and say, "No, you're great."

This is why Hebrews 12 has been such an encouragement to me. I go to it when I'm hurt, disappointed, surprised or when something goes wrong or others criticize me. It has helped me face criticism and learn from it. It also has helped me avoid bitterness. Bitterness is a major problem in our society. It has driven countless marriages apart and creates conflict between races, classes and cultures.

I have a close friend who confessed recently, "Phil, I've been bitter in my marriage. I couldn't have children. Things went wrong. I harbored bitterness because of it. Basically I've had a lousy attitude around the household." She admitted she had killed the marriage but desperately wanted it back: "What's past is past. I want to go forward."

> # "See to it that no one comes short of the grace of God; that no root of bitterness springing up causes trouble, and by it many be defiled."
> ## —Hebrews 12:15

As I sat and talked with this woman and her husband, I grieved over the wedge between them. He is a Christian; I believe with all my heart he knows the Lord. But he had given up and was bailing out on the marriage, even though she now was willing to change. They went through a torturous, painful situation, afloat on a sea of bitterness.

That didn't justify what he was doing, which was breaking up what God put together. If he persisted in this disastrous course, he would bear the consequences of that decision.

No matter what has gone wrong, God loves us and wants to restore us. If two people can turn to one another and say, "I'm really sorry; I love you unconditionally and want to make it right," all the other stuff will go away.

I can't overemphasize the seriousness of the situation. We're in the midst of a crisis. Marriages in the church, made up of people who claim to know and love Christ, are falling apart faster than those of nonbelievers. In one city, three of the top leaders in a national ministry recently blew out their marriages. There aren't simple solutions. But bitterness plants seeds of dynamite that explode like land mines as people cross them.

Daily Decisions

Late one December we were driving home from the Annual Underwear Exchange in St. Louis. Never heard of that? It's where you have over two dozen members of one extended family pile into a four-bedroom house to celebrate Christmas. A steady diet of this would be hard to handle, but for a week it's some of the most enjoyable times we've ever known.

The problem is that with only one washing machine to handle the mob of laundry generated by twenty-five folks, you rarely go home with the same stuff you brought. It could take weeks to sort out what belongs to whom and return it to its owner. Finally I started taking a big bag full of underwear to keep all of mine in one place. Then I wash them at home.

It's a great time for the family to be together, but it comes during a crush of events. When I was practicing law, our fiscal year-end was December 31. In the midst of Christmas parties, New Year's celebrations and visiting relatives, we scrambled to pay bills, calculate bonuses and make personnel decisions. December was a pressurized month. We tried to balance books, call partners and sort out year-end details. As a consequence, I always went home tired from our Christmas get-togethers.

This particular year Susy and I had another issue simmering that threatened to cause problems. It had started six months earlier as Susy and I were discussing plans to begin a Bible study in our new ministry room. We're both planners. We like to resolve details and set our schedules so we can get things done. (With six children, this is a must.) The problem is we don't always land on the same page.

Six months before Christmas, I declared, "We need to make plans. Let's get going." I wrote a letter of invitation and had the addresses ready to mail to our prospects for a fall study that would run from October through December.

"I'm really not sure," Susy said. "I'm just not ready yet."

When she listed her reasons and pointed out how crowded that season of year would be, I grunted, "OK, the Bible study is off." Charging off like a bull, I went ahead and lined up plans for the fall and the first five months of the next year. Or so I thought.

On the way home from St. Louis, Susy said, "OK, let's get our calendars out. Let's see. We're going to plan the Bible study for January, February and March."

"What?" I said. "I can't do that. There's no way."

"Well, you put it on your Day Timer."

I looked. Sure enough, it was there. But I had forgotten and made so many other plans that I didn't know how to squeeze everything into one life. Now, neither of us was upset. We just had a miscommunication. No apology was needed since neither of us had been unreasonable.

Yet the question still loomed: "OK, now what are we going to do?"

How many of you have choices like that? What are we going to do, honey? Buy this house? Sell this one? Move here or there? Do we take a vacation in June so we can attend our family reunion, or July so we can visit old friends in Florida?

So often disputes in otherwise happy, well-adjusted homes aren't over your spouse going to a bar and getting drunk. Scripture clearly says not to do that. The question many of us grapple with is, *What about these daily, nitty-gritty dilemmas?* They may sound simple but can become powder kegs.

> "Hear my cry, O God; give heed to my prayer. From the end of the earth I call to You when my heart is faint; lead me to the rock that is higher than I."
> —Psalm 61:1-2

We found the answer through prayer. The next morning I still wasn't sure what to do. So the two of us stretched out on the floor to pray. We prayed through every reason why God would want us to lead the Bible study, what He would accomplish, my schedule, the purpose for our new ministry room and our goals. Finally I realized clearly that I needed to make room for the Bible study, which proved to be a tremendous blessing.

The answer here wasn't to square off and play tug-of-war. It wasn't a question of who was right or wrong, or who would "win." We had to seek God's way. When He provided the answer, there was no arguing over which way to go, and both of us were pleased with the results. Relationships are not about winning wars. They're about love, understanding, sharing and growing together. With God in the center, they can always be successful.

Questions for Reflection

1. With whom do you need to make amends? How can you take the first step? What unresolved pain from the past is holding you back?
2. How do you discipline your children? How do you try to make it a learning experience?
3. Explain how your family confronts troublesome issues within your home. How could you improve?
4. Recall a situation where you wound up in difficult circumstances. What did you learn?
5. Have you ever apologized to your mate or children? What was the outcome?
6. What can you do to eliminate bitterness in your home?

Chapter Five
STRATEGIC HOMES

—————— Susy Downer

I'll never forget the story I heard one night at our church about the impact that we can have on future generations. A powerful, eloquent evangelist spoke that night. He discussed his belief that Boaz, Ruth's husband, had a major impact on his great-grandson, King David. To illustrate the power that we can have on future generations, he told a story about his own life.

When he was about fifteen, this evangelist had attended a revival meeting. During the revival he felt strongly impressed to walk down to the front. Kneeling at the altar, he recalled how tears came to his eyes as he heard God. It wasn't an audible voice, but he still got the message. The Lord told him, "Ron, I am calling you to preach for Me."

When he went home and told his mother, her eyes swelled up with tears of joy.

"I've never told you this," she said. "When you were just a few months old my dad stayed with us just shortly before he died. One day I was walking down the hall and I saw him leaning over your crib. He didn't even know I was there. He was weeping and crying out to God. He was saying, 'God, please call this little boy to preach for you.' And God answered that prayer of his heart fifteen years later."

I love this story because it's such a vivid reminder of the incredible impact of our prayers on our children, grandchildren and future generations. Parents, do you realize the God of the universe uses your prayers for your children in ways we cannot comprehend?

I think too of the damage Phil and I almost did to ourselves and future generations. If I had made the self-focused, perfectly rational (or so it seemed at the time) decision to divorce, we would have inflicted great emotional damage, both on ourselves and our future descendants. It is one of the reasons I am still eternally grateful to the Lord. He literally rescued us.

In chapter 2, Phil and I talked about what a battleground our marriage had become and how it was hanging by bare threads by the time we turned our lives over to Christ. However, although God slowly rebuilt it, we still had to endure struggles. One day, when I saw Jim Lyon, the man who had discipled Phil for three years, he asked, "How are things going?" only to be surprised when I burst into tears.

Within a week, his wife, Mary Gail, called and asked if we would like to come to their home once a week, along with another couple. They met with us weekly for three more years. Jim was a doctor on call every other night and Mary Gail a mother with four children. Still, they took time to build themselves into our lives. Honestly, I'm not sure our marriage would have survived if we hadn't had people like Jim, Mary Gail and Liane to help instill character, discipline and commitment in us.

A comment after an Easter dinner one year by another friend and mentor, Joe Coggeshall, made a lasting impact:

"Children have eternal significance." He wasn't even talking to me, but the words burned in my heart. As I rolled that truth over in my mind, I committed to live my life accordingly. Joe often spoke of the wisdom of having a 200-year perspective. Jim, Mary Gail and Liane had been modeling that concept for us for some time. The idea was that we all need to live with the awareness that our daily decisions affect our children, and their children's lives will affect their children and so on. Sure, the Lord might return during the next two centuries. But what if He doesn't?

> ## "The word of God kept on spreading; and the number of the disciples continued to increase greatly in Jerusalem, and a great many of the priests were becoming obedient to the faith."
> ## —Acts 6:7

An eternal perspective affects more than a choice to stay married. If we decide to spend our extra time and money on things instead of people, that also has repercussions for generation after generation. Resisting the pull of materialism and frantic activity requires a deliberate decision. We must resist the "gotta have more" ethic that permeates our society.

Under the influence of the godly people who taught us, we made a commitment. We wanted to have as great an impact on this world for the Lord as we could. We determined to become disciplemakers, both of our physical children and (we hoped) our spiritual children. We deter-

mined that no matter how busy life might become, we were
going to spend our time building eternal perspectives.
Starting at home.

Praying for Future Generations

Working as a lawyer and corporate officer for Delta Air
Lines was my dream job. I used to remark, only half-jokingly,
that I loved it so much I would have done it for free. As I
mentioned earlier, I kept working when Abigail and Paul
were born. But Jim, Mary Gail, Liane, Joe and others had
their impact. After Matthew arrived, I quit. I took this step
with great joy. God had convinced me to follow His will.
Without any regrets or glances back at the corporate world, I
have been at home for more than fifteen years.

It has been a privilege to spend these years guiding,
teaching and shaping young lives. When Phil and I prayed
that God would do whatever He needed to do with us, that
we could raise godly children who would live for Him, it
was pretty scary. But we decided we needed to trust Him
with everything. We had to give our children up and acknowledge they belong to Him. We are just stewards, helping to mold and protect them until they are old enough to
make their own decisions.

Of course, the first goal for each of our children under
God's guidance was that each of them would come to know
Jesus as Savior and Lord. We prayed for that constantly, using the passage from James 5:16 as our guide, "The effective prayer of a righteous man can accomplish much."

This verse was a vivid reminder that God cares about our
children and hears prayers deep within our hearts for our children. We pray for our children regularly and fervently. Some
close friends encouraged us to do this before we even had chil-

dren. They shared how they had prayed for their future children on the first night of their honeymoon. Every night they prayed they would have children who would come to know Christ, all of them. They continued to pray that way for years.

We made that our prayer too. We believe it has always been important that our children hear us call their name before the Lord. Not in just simple, rote prayers, but with emotion and deep feeling. We pray that they will be godly, that they will obey the Lord, that they will love Scripture. We pray that they will be patient and wait for the man or woman that God has for them and keep themselves pure for that time. We pray for their future spouse, who is a child somewhere. We pray for that person's purity, protection and heart for the Lord.

> The Lord may not answer your prayers for your children and grandchildren until you have left this earth. What a serious reminder of the eternal impact we can have on future generations.

Finally we pray for their future children. We pray that the next generation, and the next, will be godly and walk with the Lord. This is something we've done since they were little. I remember when Anna was about three we came home from a date and the baby-sitter said, "I couldn't believe what Anna prayed tonight. She said, 'Dear God, please make me a godwy woman with many godwy children.' "

I doubt she understood what that meant then, but she knew it was important. And it has always been one of her life's goals. We tell our children regularly that God has an exciting plan for their lives and that He has work for them to do. We tell them it's our job to prepare them for whatever that work is and to train them to listen for God's call. But it's their job to be obedient when God puts that call on their life.

Encouraging Words

Do you speak words of encouragement in your home? Do your children hear you praising each other, affirming your spouse's great worth and value? Remember, if you don't appreciate each other, you can't expect your children to follow suit. Constantly speaking uplifting words to your spouse will provide your children with feelings of love and security. And it will remind you to speak similar phrases to them.

> "Therefore encourage one another and build up one another, just as you also are doing. . . . We urge you, brethren, admonish the unruly, encourage the fainthearted, help the weak, be patient with everyone."
> —1 Thessalonians 5:11, 14

Too many parents forget their children aren't miniature adults, but young, fragile, impressionable creatures. They desperately need instruction, gentle care and security. They are counting on you to train them and show them how to live. We live in a cruel, negative, fickle world. Bombarded daily by people and events that can easily discourage them, our children need positive reinforcement.

I cannot emphasize that enough, especially for parents of toddlers. Every day you need to encourage those young hearts, praising them and lifting them up. Considering the frequency of discipline young children require, remember to balance that with praise. Otherwise the necessary correction you must deliver can turn into what seems like a constant barrage of criticism.

To even the scale, we regularly tell our children things like:

- How smart and wonderful they are;
- How grateful we are to be their parents;
- What a privilege it is to have them in our family;
- That they are handsome or beautiful.

> Children are becoming callous at a younger age today. That isn't too surprising, given the coarsening of our culture. But it is another reason why speaking encouraging words to our children is so vital to their emotional development.

If they believe that and grow up feeling really good about themselves, they will be less susceptible to peer pressure and negative attacks. This is especially important for girls. If a girl grows up feeling pretty because her daddy always tells her that, then the first time some boy tries to flatter her, it won't turn her head. She won't feel so insecure she's ready to throw herself into the arms of some guy who cares more about himself than her. She will develop a deep desire to please her family and the Lord.

One of our methods for discipling our children and their friends is called a Good News Club, a ministry of Child Evangelism Fellowship. We started one club while living in Atlanta and began another after moving to Chattanooga. (We discuss this in detail in chapter 11.)

One frightening development I've observed in leading these sessions is the decreasing age at which children are tender to the message of the gospel. It isn't difficult to understand when looking at the coarsening of our culture. This is yet another reason that encouragement remains so vital.

It is also why I see investing in children as so vital. Reaching children when they are still tenderhearted will vastly increase the numbers who come to Christ. Surveys repeatedly show a majority of people who accept Jesus as Savior do so before the age of eighteen. From a business standpoint, your return on investment will never be greater. Not to mention that if you give your children a vision when they are young, they will have something to hold on to for the rest of their lives.

Encouragement includes more than kind words. We use role-playing to train our children to face future decisions. Phil has been particularly good at this, especially when they were very young. He would say something like, "Let's say I'm old and sick and God's called you to Africa to be a missionary. But I say, 'Oh, no, please stay home! You've got to stay home and take care of me.' What will you do?" Of course, they knew the right answer was, "Oh, Daddy, we'll obey God."

But he wouldn't stop there. He would add, "But what if I say, 'No, you don't understand. I have spent my whole life helping you. Look at all the things I've done and given to you.' What are you going to do?"

They learned to repeat, "Oh, Daddy, we'll obey God."

Then he'd say, "What if I really want you to be a missionary? That is what I want for your life, but God says you're supposed to be a missionary to the business world and be a business owner right here. What will you do?"

They would smile, "Oh, Daddy, we'll be a business owner."

This may sound childish, but even at a young age we tried to train them to think through issues that they may encounter one day. Maybe we won't be as strong then as we are now. We have found that it has been helpful to talk through some of these concerns.

> "You shall not worship them or serve them; for I, the LORD your God, am a jealous God, visiting the iniquity of the fathers on the children, on the third and the fourth generations of those who hate Me, but showing lovingkindness to thousands, to those who love Me and keep My commandments."
> —Exodus 20:5-6

Parents, you may not believe it, but this applies to the nitty-gritty reality that confronts your children at school, on the playground and in the streets every day. Surveys have also shown children are less inclined to use drugs when their parents talk to them about it. As they mature, role-playing can help young people avoid accepting a marijuana joint, chugging down a beer at a party or "making out" just because others around them are doing it.

Godly Male Role Model

A sad truth of Scripture is how few good role models it contains for fathers. If being a good father was easy, there wouldn't be such a dearth of them in the Bible. Yet recently in my Bible study I discovered a wonderful exception. It can be found in the thirty-fifth chapter of Jeremiah. In the story, God asked Jeremiah to bring the Rechabites to a room and offer them wine. Their response follows:

> But they said, "We will not drink wine, for Jonadab the son of Rechab, our father, commanded us, saying, 'You shall not drink wine, you or your sons, forever. You shall not build a house, and you shall not sow seed and you shall not plant a vineyard or own one; but in tents you shall dwell all your days, that you may live many days in the land where you sojourn.'
>
> "We have obeyed the voice of Jonadab the son of Rechab, our father, in all that he commanded us, not to drink wine all our days, we, our wives, our sons or our daughters, nor to build ourselves houses to dwell in; and we do not have vineyard or field or seed. We have only dwelt in tents, and have obeyed and have done according to all that Jonadab our father commanded us." (Jeremiah 35:6-10)

Talk about the blessings of a good father! They said, "No thanks, we don't drink. He told us not to build houses or plant crops and vineyards and to live in tents. And if we did that, we would live a long, good life. So we've done that. We've obeyed him." No compromise with the political correctness of their day. They didn't care what others were doing or how far others strayed from God's instruction. They followed Dad's example—and he followed the Lord.

God's response follows:

"The words of Jonadab the son of Rechab, which he commanded his sons not to drink wine, are observed. So they do not drink wine to this day, for they have obeyed their father's command. But I have spoken to you again and again; yet you have not listened to Me.

"Also I have sent to you all My servants the prophets, sending them again and again, saying: 'Turn now every man from his evil way and amend your deeds, and do not go after other gods to worship them. Then you will dwell in the land which I have given to you and to your forefathers; but you have not inclined your ear or listened to Me. Indeed, the sons of Jonadab the son of Rechab have observed the command of their father which he commanded them, but this people has not listened to Me.'

"Therefore thus says the Lord, the God of hosts, the God of Israel, 'Behold, I am bringing on Judah and on all the inhabitants of Jerusalem all the disaster that I have pronounced against them; because I spoke to them but they did not listen, and I have called them but they did not answer.' "

Then Jeremiah said to the house of the Rechabites, "Thus says the LORD of hosts, the God of Israel, 'Because you have obeyed the command of Jonadab your father, kept all his commands and done according to all that he commanded you; therefore thus says the LORD of hosts, the God of Israel, "Jonadab the son of Rechab shall not lack a man to stand before Me always." ' "
(Jeremiah 35:14-19)

Can you imagine the respect that Jonadab commanded to have his sons obey his instructions? The *Life Application Bible* says that Jonadab lived more than 200 years before this incident. For two centuries the generations after Jonadab had obeyed his commandment. That is amazing to me. It was amazing to God. He grieved over Israel's corresponding lack of obedience during this time period.

I think about the relationship that man must have had with his sons that they would respect him enough to obey something so difficult. Abstaining from wine is one thing. But refusing to build houses and indulge in the material pleasures others ran after? That took strength. Yet look at their reward: Someone in that family would worship God forever.

> Fathering isn't an easy task. Otherwise, there would be more good role models available in the Bible. This is a job that requires more skill than any professional occupation on earth.

Can you imagine anything more precious than God telling you that someone from your lineage would worship Him forever? That means right now somewhere in the 6 billion people on earth there is a descendant of Rechab and Jonadab worshiping God. Isn't that exciting? That is the power of godliness in our families. What a heritage for our children's children's children's children's children!

This is the kind of role model we can all aspire to, but especially fathers. Some great men in biblical history failed miserably in this regard. The first father, Adam, lost Abel to Cain's rage. Eli's sons disgraced him and the temple. David was called a man after God's own heart, yet his children showed a lack of respect for him and some rebelled against him. Fathering isn't an easy job, and you don't get a second chance. Ask God for the wisdom needed to complete the task.

Teaching Tools

There are so many things we want to share and teach our children that it sometimes seems overwhelming. I'm sure you know the feeling. But we have discovered some valuable tools that have helped us train and disciple them. One we discovered at (of all places) a home show. We rounded the corner after looking at tile and other furnishings and there was a whole rack of *Your Story Hour* tapes.

These Bible and character-building tapes were one of the best investments we ever made. They include more than 500 stories. We've had them since our oldest child, Abigail, was four. The kids listen to them constantly—at mealtime, traveling, before going to bed, early in the morning or while they're cleaning their rooms. They have listened to each one dozens of times. This collection has really shaped their character.

The series covers wonderful stories that make the Bible come alive, missionary stories, profiles of American heroes and various issues. Some of the most helpful have been tapes that raise character issues, such as being diligent. You can say to your child, "Be diligent," but it's hard to get that across. You can model it and discipline them for a lack of diligence. But they can better grasp a story about someone who shows diligence or doesn't, and the natural consequences of each choice.

The tapes have several dozen character qualities that they're trying to build into children as they share these stories. And, parents, you will enjoy them as much as your youngsters. One friend came to me and said, "You've been telling me for years I need to get these for my grandchildren. I finally did. I got one set of twelve. I thought, *I know Susy said they were good, but I'm just going to listen to them one time to make sure be-*

fore I give them away. Well, they were so good I had to listen to them a second time before I could give them away."

One series is an eight-tape set entitled *Acts of the Apostles*. When Paul was about five, he listened to the series three times in two weeks. One afternoon as we were driving in the car, he was really quiet. I asked, "What are you thinking about, Paul?" He said, "Well, I was just thinking if I had to face death like my namesake did, would I be strong enough in Jesus not to deny Him?" The Scripture from those tapes had saturated his mind and made a strong impact.

> Jesus recognized the effectiveness of storytelling. Why do you think He used so many parables to get His points across? People could relate to them much easier than a lecture on right and wrong.

I believe that one of our main responsibilities as parents is to attempt every day to put the world in a Christ-centered perspective for our children, using whatever method is available. In your morning quiet time, ask the Lord to bring to your mind spiritual applications for the things that happen in your day. The Holy Spirit will do this for you. Ask God to also help your child to learn to think as a Christian thinks. They can do this at a young age and the sooner they start the easier it will be.

Another good training tool is to get children to read Christian biographies. One of the saddest things to me is the heroes young people have today. Even Christian youth tend to follow people from the sports and entertainment fields. There are some fine people in those areas, but there are also so many godly men and women in our history who have walked with God, and we have so much to learn from them.

There are many different ways your children can learn about such people. For example, Moody Bible Institute has a wonderful series of tapes called *Stories of Great Christians*. They're on the radio, as are *Your Story Hour* tapes, but we could never manage to tune in to those fifteen-minute segments every day. We would miss a couple and the story became disjointed, so we ordered them directly from Moody.

> "This book of the law shall not depart from your mouth, but you shall meditate on it day and night, so that you may be careful to do according to all that is written in it; for then you will make your way prosperous, and then you will have success."
> —Joshua 1:8

If you buy them, be sure to start your children on them at a young age. They were done in the 1950s and have old-fashioned organ music. If you wait too long, your kids will roll their eyes and think, *Oh, brother*. You will get to the point where you can fast-forward through the music and get to the meat of the stories.

They include tales of many godly people whom I never learned about growing up. They're fairly expensive, so think about enlisting several friends to pitch in to buy a set. You can pass them around or even get together and listen to some as a group. Take them on trips and make them a part of your children's education, especially if you homeschool. They're every bit as important as any other subject. Some are a bit dry, so you may want to get recommendations from your group about the ones their children really enjoyed. There is so much that we need to teach our children from these people's lives. These are the people we want them to model.

I also encourage listening to Christian radio. Getting young children to listen to Christian stations develops a good habit. When you're cooking dinner or have a break when the family's all together, tune in some of the great preachers of our era. Listen to Chuck Colson's commentaries on current issues, James Dobson's views on various family topics or Larry Burkett's tips on money management. Our children have learned so much from listening to radio without giving it a second thought. It is entertainment for them because they just grew up with it and listening was natural.

Be careful about the music you listen to on these stations. Some just play a lot of rock music, which I don't favor. I realize there are a wide variety of opinions about music. Just remember that beautiful, melodious Christian music is a blessing in the home. It brings peace and joy and has a calming effect. Listening to positive alternatives will help train your children to have good taste in music and entertainment.

Don't overlook another valuable resource: you. Take time to explain the gospel to your children regularly. Don't oversimplify it, such as saying everybody needs to ask Jesus into their heart. That's true, but they need to understand that they are sinners and Jesus saves sinners. They need to understand why they need a Savior, that Jesus was perfect in every way, and therefore could be a substitute for us and pay the penalty for our sin. They also need to grasp the importance of confession and repentance. A child needs to understand certain basics before he or she is ready to receive Christ.

Nurturing at Home

After our early years as Christians and once we had rebuilt our relationship, Phil and I focused on others. We started using some basic Bible studies and other tools to teach the Word. Sometimes we hosted dinner parties in our home, inviting friends and either sharing our testimony or asking someone else to speak. Then we invited those who were interested to follow up with a basic Bible study called *First Steps*, which is now the first book of Operation Timothy.

We also got involved in discipleship, mentoring people one-on-one. As our children arrived, our heart turned primarily to discipling them. Of course, since Phil still worked outside the home, he still had a Timothy. But I felt my primary job lay in discipling our children. I just didn't think I had time to use our home for ministry as I had before.

Then one spring Phil and I went on a couples' retreat. We sensed a challenge that weekend that the Lord really wanted us to do more ministry. At the time Phil, was teaching in the singles' department at church. He had a very large single-adult class of people in their early to mid-twenties. There were so many of these young people who really wanted to be discipled. Sadly, in a church of thousands, there weren't people willing to do it.

So we started an "Operation Timothy" in our home. What fun! Every Monday night we hosted these young people, most working in their first professional job. After Phil shared with the large group, we had small group discussions. We included our children in them. At seven, Abigail sat with one of the ladies' groups to discuss Phil's topic. Even three-year-old Matthew listened, although one night he fell asleep and tumbled off the chair in the middle of Phil's message.

After six months, we had a group of people so excited about sharing their faith with their friends that they wanted to have an outreach. They knew that they needed to reach some people if they were going to have someone to disciple. So they planned a special dinner at our home. They got very excited, inviting their friends and coworkers. They also insisted that you couldn't attend unless you brought someone who didn't know the Lord.

> "How blessed is the man who does not walk in the counsel of the wicked, nor stand in the path of sinners, nor sit in the seat of scoffers! But his delight is in the law of the LORD, and in His law he meditates day and night."
> —Psalm 1:1-2

An even greater thrill was watching the impact this process made on our children. We walked around our neighborhood and handed out invitations to the parents of many of their friends. Then the children would pray for them.

The night of the barbecue came and it was a wonderful evening. We invited a bluegrass band, which was a big hit, and Phil and I shared our story. We closed with prayer and an invitation to receive Christ. We had distributed cards where people could indicate that they had prayed to receive Christ so we would know how to follow up with them.

After all the guests had left and we returned all the tables and chairs we borrowed from church, we gathered to look at the cards, excited to see who had marked a card that they had prayed to receive Christ. Finally I took the kids up to bed.

"Paul," I said to our then-five-year-old son, "it's 11 o'clock. I know you're too tired to pray. You can go on to sleep."

"No, Mama, I want to pray," he said. Then, bowing his head, he said, "God, I just want to ask that all those people who didn't accept You tonight would get another chance."

I had to apologize to the Lord that night, telling Him, "I didn't think I had time for home ministry because I was discipling my children, but if I really want them to catch a vision for giving their lives away to others, I don't have time *not* to open my home for ministry. Thank you for showing me that."

I leave you with this question: Are your children seeing God's witness in your home?

Questions for Reflection

1. List all the activities that occupy your time during the week. What could you give up to allow you time to disciple a young Christian?
2. What self-centered decisions have you made in the past that you now regret? What can you do to resolve this situation?
3. Did you have a parent, grandparent or other relative who prayed for you? What are you doing to pass that blessing on?
4. What things are you doing to encourage your spouse? Your children?

5. List three steps you can take to teach your children about biblical characters and historical Christian figures.

6. How can you make your home a place where God's presence is apparent?

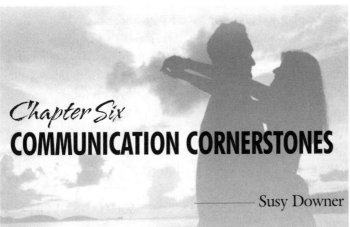

Chapter Six
COMMUNICATION CORNERSTONES

———— Susy Downer

Does your spouse read the newspaper while you're trying to carry on a conversation? Or pull out a needlepoint kit and nod occasionally, leaving you wondering if your partner heard a word you said? Chances are you get pretty upset—unless you enjoy talking to a blank wall. Communication isn't a one-way street, and it is vital not just for your marriage, but if you hope to raise children to make an eternal impact.

After Phil and I accepted Christ and set out to rebuild our marriage, we learned that to succeed we had to improve our communication skills. As we struggled through shedding old habits and healing the wounds they caused, better communication increased our depth of understanding for each other. We were less likely to fly off the handle and attack each other when we grasped our partner's attempts to change.

For example, Phil had a desire to work at improving his temper. So he drew up plans and set out to accomplish them. Believe me, it isn't easy reversing a thirty-year pattern of exploding to relieve anger, stress and frustration.

But he planned and improvised, going as far as to rate himself on how nice he had been to me on a particular day.

That didn't automatically smooth things over. We had so many ups and downs we felt like we lived on a roller coaster. Yet when I saw his efforts it helped me admire and appreciate my husband's desire to change. It made me more patient when he slipped and lost his cool over something. That tempered my reaction when normally I would have gotten pretty upset with him.

> Do you remember how excited you used to get when you were getting ready to go on a date? Scrubbing, cleaning, primping, dressing up and putting your best foot forward for that special person? Why should it be any different now that you're married?

Our weekly dates were a key in mending our fractured relationship. There is no substitute for one-on-one time. At first Phil had a hard time convincing me they were necessary. This was before we had any children, so it wasn't like we were trying to escape bedlam at home or the constant clutches of little fingers. Plus we were in the midst of rehabilitating an old house. Besides the expense, that requires plenty of time.

I was satisfied if we sat next to each other and talked while scraping paint off a baseboard. But Phil needed my full attention, looking him in the eye and listening to what he said. Once we had children, I was grateful we had established that pattern. Those times of casual conversation and dreaming dreams are crucial to any couple.

You may be tempted to turn your dates into a "business meeting," discussing upcoming trips or plans for household repairs. This is especially true when your calendars stay full, as ours do. Now, it is perfectly permissible to talk about your children if that's a particularly pressing need in your home. But I believe it's best if you concentrate on how you're doing with each other.

One reason for date time is that no matter how long a couple has been married, they struggle with adjustments and the need to forgive each other for intemperate outbursts, neglect or thoughtlessness.

In our case, Phil had a lot of damage to repair and communication was the tool of reconciliation. His fits of anger had shocked me and frozen my emotions. Naturally this had an impact on our physical relationship.

But not all the blame belonged to Phil. I also had issues to resolve. I grew up in a wonderful, peaceful home, but one where deep feelings just weren't discussed. So I had absolutely no preparation for being honest about intimate subjects. That proved to be the source of additional arguments. But when I saw Phil's rock-solid commitment to being faithful and teaching our children about the need for purity, I realized I needed to do my part.

This caused spiritual and marital growth. Much of it occurred during those times when we shut the world out to focus on each other. Phil had to acknowledge the serious damage he had caused and prove he was serious about changing. I saw my need to become more affectionate—creative in the area of our physical relationship—and loving. I decided that he deserved that, simply because he was my husband. We had made a vow to love each other for a lifetime, and that means giving our best. I don't want you to think we're special or trying to sound like the all-American couple. But we have reaped the benefits that are available to any couple who will make the effort to communicate and grow together.

A tragedy I have observed, especially among Christians, is the large number of women who just don't take the subject of the physical relationship seriously enough. There are many husbands who are trying to be faithful and loving to their wife and put her at the top of their priority list. But that is very difficult for a man if his wife isn't giving herself to him in an enthusiastic manner. For the wife, improving the marriage may not rank in her top ten if it requires her to serve her husband physically, beyond her own personal needs.

> Not every man who falls morally
> is solely to blame for his failure.
> He may have had a wife who
> didn't take her responsibility to
> their marriage very seriously.

Wives might never admit it publicly, but they often don't make the effort—just as I didn't for so long. These women fail to realize they are blocking their husband's efforts to be godly and pure by not doing what God wants them to do and pushing themselves out of their comfort zones. We ought to be so exciting for our husbands that they're not tempted by the women throwing themselves at them.

Christians sometimes wear blinders to what goes on in society. Whether you're aware of it or not, there are women in nearly every workplace who make themselves available to any husband who is looking to stray. The aggressive ones may tempt him. Christian wives hold the key to their spouse's ability to withstand that.

I heard well-known pastor and author Chuck Swindoll say several years ago that he started keeping a list of Christian leaders—not people in his church but well-known men—who had fallen morally. His list back then was up around 235. We focus on the men, but I think it's safe to say the wife often (though not always) played a role in the situation.

When it comes to improving your communication, don't neglect talking with the Lord. He was working with Phil and I through our difficult times, drawing us together. We prayed about it often and watched Him answer right before our eyes. Don't hesitate to ask God for help in the physical area of your marriage. He invented it and cares about it too.

Besides improving your marriage, there is another vital reason to improve communication, maintain a healthy physical relationship and iron out your difficulties as a couple: Your children are watching you. What you do leaves a more lasting impression than what you say. Those who stick together and work out those tough interpersonal problems are teaching their children invaluable lessons about life and modeling how they should persevere in their own marriages one day. Life on this earth is full of pain, anger and disappointment. But those who work through it realize the joy and great reward of perseverance.

Raising Disciples

Fortunately Phil and I didn't have any children as we began the process of repairing our marriage. But as we grew in our faith and began having children, raising them to become disciples—and disciplers—soon occupied one of the

top spots on our list of priorities. While we are primarily
addressing marriage in this book, children are such a crucial part of marriage that I felt the need to address their
role in your marriage—and the need for them to be part of
a family-centered ministry.

One of the ironies of writing about family-centered ministry is that Phil's jobs have frequently required travel. But we
have found that good communication and the effort to use
these absences as opportunities help us remain in balance.

> # While traveling does put a strain on togetherness as a couple and as a family, with careful planning you can keep the lines of communication open.

Over the years, Phil has periodically taken one of our
children on his trips. This gives them one-on-one time and
is part of his discipling of each child. It has also given each
of them a vision for our ministry and getting involved in
other people's lives. Sure, there are negatives. In one sense,
travel fragments the family, but we're grateful it isn't at a
continual, unrelenting pace.

When Phil was still practicing law and was gone from
home even more, the children and I constantly prayed for
him. He told us what he was doing and how we could help
support him. When he moved into full-time ministry, our
family took on those concerns. We share his burdens, are
aware of his challenges and continually pray for him. His
frequent phone calls back home keep the lines of communication open.

Phil often told the children part of their job was to be
obedient to me while he was away. He warned them that if

he got a report they were giving Mom a problem because he was out of town and couldn't come home and discipline them, then he would quit his job. They appreciate that we are part of a team. Their part is at home.

If God has called the father into a ministry that separates him from the family more than would be ideal, be careful to stay in balance. Out of necessity, we have seasons where we consciously limit outside activities to spend more time at home. Pray for balance and make sure you get plenty of time together when Dad is at home. When Phil comes home from a trip, he has a date lined up for each of the seven of us individually. It may be getting an ice cream cone down the street, but everyone gets one to two hours of one-on-one time to renew their relationship.

We believe our most effective ministry as a family is hosting people in our home. That might mean a Bible club for neighborhood children or adult Bible studies. We make our children part of each. Many families have Bible studies in their home, but put the kids to bed early so they can "do ministry." I believe that is missing out on an incredible opportunity. It is amazing what children can learn if they're involved. They can serve, greet people and develop skills in interacting with adults. During studies they learn to sit still and listen to the teaching.

Don't be surprised if you try this and encounter resistance. This isn't a popular concept (and may be inappropriate in some small group contexts where very personal burdens may be shared). But one reason we have done it is that it fits with a question we are always asking ourselves: "How can we give our family a vision for ministry?"

We believe getting children involved with adults in Bible study is helping to groom them to lead such studies later in life. It also does wonders for our family's devotional times, as questions from these sessions lead to further discussions.

Besides trying to develop a ministry vision, one thing that has been helpful to us is to have a family life purpose. This helps us filter requests for our time outside the home. We know in our family that the Lord has called us to evangelism and discipleship. So when someone from church desperately needs somebody to teach children's Sunday school, we don't automatically say yes.

> "Now, little children, abide in Him, so
> that when He appears, we may have
> confidence and not shrink away from
> Him in shame at His coming. If you
> know that He is righteous, you
> know that everyone also who practices
> righteousness is born of Him."
> —1 John 2:28-29

There is no doubt some could come to know the Lord in such a class and be discipled. But there are other people who can do that and we would tend to say that doesn't fit where the Lord has given us our specific vision. So then we can say, "No, we'd love to do it but we can't." We can say that without guilt because we have a clear standard against which to measure requests.

Teaching a Work Ethic

God has a pattern established in Luke 16:10: "He who is faithful in a very little thing is faithful also in much; and he who is unrighteous in a very little thing is unrighteous also in much." Establishing good communication with your spouse is the first step in faithfully guiding your family. You can't communicate with your children if you can't handle it with your mate.

Communication is vital to a balanced, happy family. You can't hope for a good marriage if you can't talk with your mate. And you can't teach your children if they can't understand what you're trying to get across. There are many valuable lessons you can teach your children, beginning with a good work ethic.

One of the greatest crimes American society commits against children today is letting them take it too easy. Children can't be expected to develop discipline and a work ethic unless they learn hard work and responsibility at a young age. And you can't hope they will learn it unless you and your spouse first agree on the necessity of this lesson. (Moms, hear me. You will be the first to let your little ones take a pass on hard work.)

Each of our children learned to work at a young age, helping with cleaning the house and cooking the food. The tasks they learn at home are helping prepare them for sharing in family ministry.

Some master routines faster than others. Our son Paul adapted quickly. On the other hand, Matthew is a "people person" who struggled with learning to complete a task without getting distracted. The rest of our children fall somewhere in between.

However, by training them and helping them develop a focus early in life, we got help a lot sooner than many families. We expect a lot of our children. Guess what? None of them died from overwork. Children rise to the level of expectations placed on them. They want a challenge. They want to learn. They want to dream huge dreams. Granted, they have to put forth the effort, but it is up to parents to teach them the discipline that will point them in the right direction.

As you might suspect, we encountered opposition. Especially when they were little, family members said, "You just expect so much." I disagree. Sometimes I think we don't expect enough. We started with chore books when the children were pre-kindergartners. We used a photograph album where the plastic flips up on each side. We placed large index cards in each section listing what they should do every day. They had a china marker (which could be wiped off the plastic each day) to check things off as they completed them.

That kept things under control. Lose control of a house full of children and you are courting disaster. Among their duties is cooking. We started them young and they enjoyed it. I have never placed a huge priority on meals. None of us is starving, and we eat balanced meals, but over the last few years, the children have done more and more of the cooking. Our oldest child, Abigail, loves to cook. Everyone was thrilled when her turn came. When she began college and didn't have time to cook, the other children teased her that everyone lost weight.

Over time we became very organized with our meal plans. This called for advance planning during the week. By Friday everyone had to tell Abigail what his or her meal would be and give her a list of needed ingredients. She would check the cupboards, put together a list, and then I would go shopping. I have other drivers now, which makes it easier to get all the groceries.

Sometimes this has called for lowering our expectations of meals. But that's fine with me. It has saved me lots of time and released me to do other things. Plus it is preparing our children for the future, including our sons. Boys used to be raised with the idea that cooking was "women's work." But nothing is sadder than a young bachelor who shells out a fortune on expensive prepared microwave dinners because he never learned to boil an egg.

Setting the kitchen in order is just one of the areas we attack in our home. We also insist our children organize their closets and drawers. What a challenge that has been. Children don't particularly care about neatness. Nevertheless, we assign cabinets and drawers to each child and then have periodic inspections. The more often we have inspections, the better the accountability.

> ## "But all things must be done properly and in an orderly manner."
> ## —1 Corinthians 14:40

Accountability is the key for keeping the house from looking like a disaster area. This may sound like we're trying to relive Phil's military service. Well, how many of you would appreciate more order at home? How many of your children would be able to find things and complete their homework because they know where their pens, pencils, notebooks and papers are? Do your children frantically search through piles of debris to find their schoolwork?

In a fit of honesty, our son Joshua admitted he wouldn't mind more frequent inspections. We had one of these weeks where everybody got his or her closet cleaned and yanked all the hidden toys, books and games from under the bed. Dad was going to do inspection. After I did this three days in a row, Joshua said, "Mom, I'll probably be sorry I said this later, but if Dad would just do inspection every day, I know my room would be a lot neater."

We're still struggling, as you probably are. Consistently keeping up with these disciplines is difficult, but it is still our goal. Orderly children mature faster into disciplined, orderly adults who are more dedicated to doing ministry in Christ's name.

Sibling Squabbles

Did we have squabbles and sibling rivalries in our home? You bet! (Sometimes it felt like watching replays of Phil and myself from our early days of marriage.) How did we deal with our children's interruptions and siblings fighting with each other? A lot of patience and attempts to resolve problems so they didn't constantly flare into even worse conflicts.

Children can fight without any encouragement. Sibling rivalry is part of human nature. But how much of the conflict in your home stems from the battles between you and your spouse? Children imitate what they see, and very effectively. Don't pick at your mate and excuse that away as "blowing off steam." Your children will take the habit to extremes.

Modeling patience with your mate will teach your children proper behavior. And it will give you the stamina to deal with the outbursts and interruptions that are part of children's growing up. As for the interruptions, a friend told us once of a practice they use that made so much sense we immediately put it to use.

Try this: When a child wants to say something, just encourage him to come over, put a hand on your knee or shoulder and stand there quietly until you recognize him. With our older children, we have had them come and just stand there. It is easy to see them in our peripheral vision and we know they want our attention.

I would like to say that each time they patiently waited until we acknowledged them. But the truth is it took a while to accomplish that. But we discovered this is an excellent way to train them not to interrupt.

> "Therefore if you are presenting your offering at the altar, and there remember that your brother has something against you, leave your offering there before the altar and go; first be reconciled to your brother, and then come and present your offering."
> —Matthew 5:23-24

When the children were younger, fighting was the hardest problem I faced at home. Nothing grieved me more then dealing with bickering among our children. I marveled when I read articles where people said they just didn't allow it in their home. I thought, *How do you not allow it?* That was our goal, but we didn't always reach it.

What we did fairly successfully prohibit was name-calling, belittling and negative attacks. Nothing bruises feelings easier or shuts down communication faster than personal slights. Granted, we were not perfect on this score. We had the avid gum chewers and those who called them "Gum breath." If we pointed that out, the offender would say,

"That's not a name. I'm just saying, 'Oh, the gum breath. I can't stand it.' "

Sometimes it was like watching ranchers battle farmers, or sheep herders versus cattlemen. Things like, "You're too close to me because you're chewing gum," which brought the response, "Well, I haven't chewed gum for three days," or some other snappy retort.

> "Now all these things are from God, who reconciled us to Himself through Christ and gave us the ministry of reconciliation, namely, that God was in Christ reconciling the world to Himself, not counting their trespasses against them, and He has committed to us the word of reconciliation."
> —2 Corinthians 5:18-19

The principle we are trying to teach them is to think of others more than themselves. Since I'm home all day, this is usually my responsibility. With two in college, three of high school age and one elementary student, I am grateful to say that our perseverance paid off. The bickering has diminished considerably (I didn't say disappeared). But for many years it seemed like I was constantly asking things like, "Were your words a blessing to your brother?" That usually brought a hang-dog look and the grudging admission, "Well, no."

So often—and do you think they learn this from watching adults in action?—children think they're justified, regardless of the argument or whatever the circumstances. They only see their side. They think they are *so right*. Many times I tried to referee these disputes, and after listening to both sides sometimes I still couldn't decide who was right, either. You will wear yourself out trying to settle every dispute. Encourage them to settle things on their own, but if one of the pair always seems to "win," you may have to intervene.

We have assigned Bible verses trying to teach them the right way to settle arguments. One day as we were packing to attend a conference, some petty issue arose and set sparks flying. I reminded the boys, "Guys, remember what we talked about during Bible study about reconciliation? This is it. Knowing the theory doesn't do any good. Apply it right now."

"Oh, yeah," one of them mumbled.

Such disputes demand constant patience and effort. Any parent gets frayed nerves. But no matter how frustrating, it is a matter of sticking with them, knowing that sooner or later the teaching will pay dividends. They won't learn overnight. We try to handle petty bickering by first stopping them. Once we calm the situation, we talk about why they were irritable and try to reason with them.

When the boys were young, an argument sometimes broke into a fistfight. Phil would order them to do pushups. He didn't let them off easy, either. The first offense called for 100 pushups. If they fought again, he told them to do another 100 pushups. Sometimes he would come home and have to deal with the aftermath of a severe argument. It could take two hours to work through it. He literally exhausted some of our children, requiring exercises like pushups and doing arm circles while holding heavy cans of tomatoes and chili beans (dubbed "chilis").

We believe "chilis" is a particularly effective alternative to spanking boys with a lot of excess energy. We are now seeing the fruit of years of giving them biblical principles, modeling the principles of loving each other and being a blessing to each other, and sticking with them. Having older children who have passed through childish stages has given us a lot of encouragement.

We also insist they apologize to each other. "I'm sorry" may be one of the hardest phrases to utter, but it is also one of the most effective. And the failure to do so can create more serious arguments weeks later. Obviously there is a difference between simply saying it and meaning it. It isn't too difficult when a child makes a quick, irritable comment that isn't that serious. We don't allow words that sound contrary to their voice and the appearance of their face. When their attitude doesn't line up with their words, the words mean nothing.

> "He who spares his rod hates
> his son, but he who loves him
> is careful to discipline him.
> —Proverbs 13:24, NIV

As a parent, you can sense when their attitude is sincerely apologetic. If it is not, don't allow mere words to get them off the hook. Persevere in your discipline or employ heart-to-heart discussions until you have achieved sincere repentance. I have spent hours on this! But in my opinion, nothing is as important in child discipline as teaching a child that he can choose to have a good attitude.

If the dispute involves some deep, heartfelt problem, we may have the two angry children go off together, talk it out, pray and forgive each other. As a last resort, we spank. If we've warned and talked and prayed and they continue to bicker, sometimes this is the only method that works. If they don't adjust their attitude and become apologetic and repentant, we may spank again. You know when you see a repentant attitude and you can't stop until you get it, or your discipline goes for naught.

Handling Money

Besides a poor work ethic, another glaring shortcoming in American households is a grip on spending. The era of easy credit has made it all too easy to get strapped to a chain of revolving payments. The average family has way too much credit card and installment debt. If this is your problem, what kind of lessons are your children picking up?

The reason I mention money is because financial pressures are one of the leading causes of divorce. Do you talk to your children about money? Many people in my parents' generation didn't. I often hear stories from people whose parents never prepared them to handle finances. They never talked about what they made or how they spent it. I attribute a lot of that to the stoic nature of their era, but I think it was a great disservice to their children.

There is not room in this book to teach lessons on balancing a budget or financial management. There are many excellent books on the market that already do that. One I recommend is *Raising Money-Smart Kids* by noted financial advisor Ron Blue and his wife, Judy. Whatever material you choose, I want to encourage you strongly to tackle this subject with them. As Christian financial counselor Larry Burkett has often noted, a student can graduate from college or university with advanced degrees and never take a course in how to balance a checkbook.

One question I am frequently asked when speaking at parenting seminars is whether we give our children an allowance. Yes. When they are in elementary and middle school we give them a small allowance. Once they are in high school we give them a little more and expect them to pay for activities they choose, like going out to dinner with a friend. That helps them learn they can't do everything. It also keeps me from being the bad guy and saying, "No, we can't afford that."

We don't tie it to work. We expect quite a lot from them around the house as part of their responsibilities of living in the home. But we feel they need some money of their own to manage. How else will they learn to handle it?

> "The priest, the son of Aaron, shall be with the Levites when the Levites receive tithes, and the Levites shall bring up the tenth of the tithes to the house of our God, to the chambers of the storehouse."
> —Nehemiah 10:38

A biblical principle we constantly stress is tithing. That comes off the top. We haven't been as strict about savings, because we're not giving them that much, anyway. While I certainly agree with the wisdom and necessity of savings, giving to the Lord's work should come first. We want our children to recognize this as a lifelong priority.

To understand how they go about tithing, you need to first understand the system I designed a few years ago. At the time, our allowances ranged from about $5 to $11 per month, with the smallest amount going to the youngest children. But that proved to be a headache with five children (our youngest was too young to get one at the time) and passing out money they weren't spending right away.

To resolve the problem, I bought a ledger book and put each of their names on a page. Then each month I would credit them with that month's allowance. The money accrued in my ledger bank just as if it were sitting in a bank account.

You would be surprised how money adds up when it's not consumed daily on candy bars, gum balls and video games. Nor could they say, "You forgot to give me my allowance." It was recorded in the book and if a month or two passed and I forgot to do it, catching up was no problem.

If they wanted to spend some of it, I'd say, "OK, put the amount in the debit column." They deducted the amount from their balance and I gave them the cash. That can be tough on your budget when you have to pay. But it was worth it because it took less time. Plus it curbed their appetite to spend money in frivolous ways. Children who don't learn how to control their appetites become adults drowning in debt.

However, even though the biblical ideal was to give the "first fruits" of their allowance, this system sometimes meant they got behind on tithing. No problem. As the calendar year came to an end and we tidied up loose ends, it was a great time for the children to figure out how to spend their tithe. In addition, they often gave much more than ten percent. Rather than calculate percentages, they just started passing out chunks of money to various ministries.

Our children were often giving twenty, thirty or forty percent of their allowance to the Lord's work. The first time I realized it I had to catch myself. I almost said, "Do you know how much you're giving?" We have always given substantially above our tithe, but we haven't reached forty percent yet.

Wow, this is great, I whispered to myself. *They're not worried about the percentage.* They were just reasoning that they had this much money available and really didn't have anything to do with it, so they would love to give it to this ministry or that missionary. When we give generously to God's work, it's like telling Him, "You know, Lord, there are a lot of ways I could spend this money. But I'm putting You first, ahead of my own desires."

I think this attitude pleases our Creator, not the amount or the percentage. Giving also opens the gateway to communication, whether to God, our mate or our children. It is one of the cornerstones for a better life.

Questions for Reflection

1. On a scale of one to ten, with ten the best score, how would you rate your communication with your spouse? What can you do to improve?
2. How does your marital communication affect your communication with your children?
3. What kind of ministry do you do as a family? If you're not doing anything, where can you start? Have you asked your pastor or missions committee how your family can serve?
4. Does travel keep you away from home regularly? What are you doing to stay in touch? What other steps can you take to improve communication with your family?
5. What chores do you assign your children? How do you follow up to make sure they're done correctly?

6. How do you resolve disputes between your children? Find three Scriptures that talk about forgiveness and reconciliation and have your children memorize them.
7. How are you teaching your children to give to the Lord's work?

Chapter Seven
TEAM BUILDING

———— Phil Downer

My friend's voice faltered, turning soft on the other end of the phone line. I couldn't believe what he was telling me. After years of marriage and what he thought was a close relationship, his wife had walked out. She told him, "I want out of this marriage" and left—lock, stock and barrel.

"You've got to be kidding," I said. I thought I was talking to the wrong person. "What do you mean, she left?"

"Well, she just left," he repeated.

"Why did she leave?"

"I don't know."

"Wait a minute. What do you mean, you don't know?"

"I have no idea," he said. "I'm a faithful husband, a Christian, a godly man. I'm involved in ministry. I bring my check home. I'm not involved in anything outside the home that's immoral. I'm always there for her. I have no idea."

A red flag waving in my mind, I protested, "Now, wait a minute. That's impossible."

"No, I have no idea," he insisted.

"Well, let me ask you a few questions. First of all, she's gone, right?"

"She left. She packed. I came home and she was gone."

"She didn't leave a note?"

"Nothing much. She just said, 'I'm out of this marriage.' "

"Have you been selfish?"

"No."

"Unfaithful?"

"No."

"Hard on her?"

"No."

> "But God has so composed the body, giving more abundant honor to that member which lacked, so that there should be no division in the body, but that the members may have the same care for one another."
> —1 Corinthians 12:24-25

"Anger?" I asked. "Do you have problems with your temper?"

"No, I don't have any of that."

"Well, let me ask you a few more questions," I said, referring to a list of ten common intimacy needs in marriage. These are needs each of us has and should strive to meet in our partner's life (as well as our children's and others close to us).

He didn't know what I was talking about, so I quickly faxed him a copy. After he had them in his hand, I continued. "There are ten needs listed on this page. I want to ask how you're doing in your marriage with these. Rate them on a scale of one to ten, with one being lousy and ten being great.

"Let's start with the first one: Attention. How are you doing with thinking about your wife and giving her the attention she needs? That's from First Corinthians 12:25, that we should care for one another. How about the second one, acceptance? Are you deliberate and ready to give favorable responses to your wife?"

He wasn't saying much, so I pressed on.

"What about number three, appreciation, meaning you give her praise? How about support and bearing her burdens? That's the fourth one. Then we have the fifth, encouragement. Do you give encouragement to your wife? Is your relationship based on encouragement and appreciation?

"What about the next one, affection? Do you express affection to her in the way she would like to receive it? How about respect? And security? Do you have a secure relationship, where she can raise questions and concerns about you and your life? Comfort's number nine. Is this a relationship where you offer comfort to one another? What about approval? Do you accept her as satisfactory?"

I paused for breath, but couldn't hear anything on the other end. Finally my friend started sobbing. "Phil, I now know why she left."

For a handy reference guide, I have listed these needs on the next page. These are some of the most powerful principles of relationships I've ever read, and not just for marriage. I use them to guide my relationships with my children and others. They are simple yet profound. An awareness of these principles can spell the difference between a family where each person lives in isolation and one that bonds into a cohesive unit.

Principles of Intimacy
(What Do You Need?)[1]

- *Acceptance.* Deliberate and ready reception; receiving a favorable response (see Romans 15:7).

- *Affection.* Care and closeness communicated through physical touch and affirming words (see Romans 16:16).

- *Appreciation.* Words and feelings of praise and personal gratefulness from your mate (see 1 Corinthians 11:2).

- *Approval.* Expressed commendation; knowing your partner thinks and speaks well of you (see Romans 14:18).

- *Attention.* Appropriate interest and support (see 1 Corinthians 12:25).

- *Comfort.* Coming alongside with words, feelings and touch to offer tenderness (see 2 Corinthians 1:3-4).

- *Encouragement.* To be urged forward and positively persuaded toward a goal (see 1 Thessalonians 5:11).

- *Respect.* To feel valued and highly regarded; to feel as though you are of great worth (see 1 Peter 2:17).

- *Security.* Confidence of harmony in a relationship and feeling free from harm or danger (see Psalm 122:7).

- *Support.* To have someone come alongside and gently help carry the load (see Galatians 6:2).

Painful Examination

One way the Lord helped Susy and I heal our marriage was through our concentration on this process. It's like having the plays listed in front of you as you head into the championship game. However, it took us years because David and Theresa Ferguson had not yet founded Intimate Life Ministries and written this list. Now that we're aware of these guidelines, we continually review them as a checkup on each other.

I remember the first time I asked Susy, "Honey, how am I doing on this list, from one to ten?" She scored me—honestly. Kind of scary, isn't it? You might think you're doing great but when those close to you score you honestly, you might rank near the bottom. Like affection. I probably deserved a score of one in Susy's eyes, but she gave me grace—about a three. I still protested, saying, "What, are you kidding? We have a great life of intimacy. It's just super."

> For several decades, feminists have tried to convince Americans that women are just as capable as men and essentially no different. I agree with the capability part, but the two genders are as different as night and day.

"Well, that's the way you express it," she replied. "But that's not my need."

Have you ever noticed that women are different from men? Their idea of affection is light years away from men's. My idea of expressing tenderness varies greatly from Susy's. She likes candlelit romance, while my focus on affection deals with physical intimacy. We're like many couples.

As I mentioned in chapter 3, it has taken us a long time to realize the extent of our differences. I've had to diligently work at understanding and resolving those that can be resolved. But as we work together, better understanding our needs, wants and gifts can be a great source of strength. It's like joining hands and locking fingers, fitting together in a strong unit. We have more power intertwined with each other than either of us would possess separately.

I have also reviewed this list with my children, asking, "On a scale of one to ten, how's Dad doing?" It is amazing what I discovered. The first reaction was one of wonderment. My children asked whether I really wanted to hear the truth. That told me a lot. Let's face it. Honesty can be very painful and create intensive conflict if one party takes offense. But resolving differences and airing feelings is better than a fragile, phony peace.

> "Children, be obedient to your parents in all things, for this is well-pleasing to the Lord. Fathers, do not exasperate your children, so that they will not lose heart."
> —Colossians 3:20-21

One of my strengths is that I'm a great analyst. I have daydreamed regularly about doing commentary on *Monday Night Football*. I wouldn't necessarily be right, but *I* would never be in doubt. At the same time, one of my weaknesses is that I'm a great analyst. Particularly when nobody wants analysis.

Take, for example, when one of our children would come running in the door, blood running from his knees, crying, "Daddy, I fell in the driveway." In the past, my response was something like, "You know, if you wore your tennis shoes and didn't run down the driveway, you wouldn't have that problem." Great analysis; bad results. What they needed was a sympathetic hug, not a lecture on their mistakes.

Being open with our children has proved to be a challenge. For example, when I went to Paul to ask him to rate me, he was about ten years old. I told him I really wanted to know how he felt. I encouraged him to tell me about his needs. After some hesitation, he said, "Well, I really have a great need for acceptance from you."

"Good, I really do," I replied. "I really appreciate you. You know you're my son. I talk about you and involve you in stuff. We go out together once a week and talk whenever possible. I tell everybody how my . . ."

Suddenly I saw Paul's eyes dropping, signaling that he was backing away. Realizing I had been defensive, I said, "Wait a minute. I'm sorry. What do you mean by acceptance? This is really an important question. What does that mean to you?"

"Well, Dad, acceptance to me is when you come down and look at my fort . . . uh . . . if you would say some positive things about my fort before you start telling me what I could have done better," he said. "Then I would feel your acceptance."

Ouch. That hurt. Who did I think I was, constantly trying to show that I have the best way of doing everything? Why was I criticizing my children for their worthwhile endeavors? What a midcourse correction that conversation caused.

It feels wonderful to come alongside them, see what they are doing and say, "Yes, that's great. Look at all those nails. Boy, they're really holding on to those boards. That's fantastic." I like to joke that the nails could be all bent over and

the boards sprouting in a dozen directions—a lawsuit waiting to happen—and the only thing the kids hear from me
will be excitement.

When he was fourteen, our rapidly maturing Paul did a
substantial amount of work on our room addition. At two
he had started out bending nails on two-by-fours in the
basement. We all have to start somewhere. I now appreciate how God wants us to be an encouragement to those
close to us and accept them the way they are. If we do, they
may listen more closely and learn some things from us.

Open Listening

It takes years to learn to listen. We get so caught up in
what we're doing, where we're going and how we're going
to get there that we forget a bunch of others around us
would like to join the venture. Part of my growth in learning to listen more closely to my family came from applying
this list of principles to relationships in the office.

I'll never forget the first time I passed out this list and asked
some of the people there to rate me. They reacted about the
same as my children: "Really? You really want us to do this?"

"Yes," I said. "I want to identify the top three needs you
have, the things you are most sensitive to and what you appreciate."

While this is a book on marriage, the reason I mention this
experience is that the same principles apply to building a
team—whether that team is your marital partner, family,
church, ministry or small group. Nobody has the same three
priorities, which is why we need to become more aware of
those around us.

One staff member gave me a high score on affection. He
commented, "You know, Phil, I really appreciate the affection."

"Well, great," I smiled.

"The only problem is I don't need affection," he said, freezing my smile in place. "I don't need all those 'atta boy's.' I don't need you to hug me. If you never hug me again, it'll be too soon, man."

"Well, what do you need?"

"I need your attention."

"Hey, I give you attention," I said, pointing out the encouragement I offer via my enthusiastic, back-slapping style.

> Taking time to listen means putting aside your plans and concentrating on what the other person has to say. Don't get defensive if he or she wants to point out a shortcoming. If you do, the other person will stop being honest and communication is lost.

"That's not attention," he said, shaking his head. "That's football. I need attention."

"What's attention? What does attention look and feel like to you?"

"Well, you don't give me attention," he said. "Working with you is like working with a train conductor on a Friday morning. You've got trains coming and going. Everybody is going in and out of the station. You're on your voice mail. You're checking your e-mail. You're dictating. Someone's coming in this way and someone else another."

Gesturing with one hand, he added, "It's like a pony express in your office. Doors are open, you're shouting this way and that. . . . I feel like I don't have your attention.

What I need from you is one hour of quiet. You listening to me, with the doors closed and you focused on me."

"I'm sorry. I'm really sorry. I guess I just had no idea how all this affected you."

Another man came in to talk over his list. This was a tough man, a military veteran. Older than me, he had been through some battles. When I asked him how I was doing, he replied, "Pretty well."

"Which one of these qualities on the list do you really need?"

> This man needed my attention, some time with my office door closed and daily interruptions put to rest. Otherwise he didn't feel he was getting what he needed. Does your mate need the same kind of devoted listening?

"I really need some mumph," he said, his voice fading on the last word to an indistinguishable mutter.

"What?"

"I really need mumph," he repeated.

"What?"

"Security."

His response puzzled me at first. But then I considered the meaning of security—freedom from exposure to danger. This was a military veteran. For years he had grappled with challenges and uncertainties on a daily basis. Now he needed to know that he was secure in his position.

"I need to be able to come to you with an idea that's not all nailed down," he continued. "I need to come to you with a problem that maybe I won't have the solution to and know that you will listen. And know that you won't try to fix it before I get it out of my mouth. And that you won't criticize me for having a problem."

> "Everyone must be quick to hear, slow to speak and slow to anger; for the anger of man does not achieve the righteousness of God." —James 1:19-20

I made notes and a purposeful plan to try to improve in these areas (and others). I learned something else through this exercise. If your spouse, children or a friend comes to you with a criticism or suggestion on how you can change for the better, your natural inclination will be to defend yourself. Or you will try to rationalize the situation. But when you throw up these roadblocks, the other person will stop being honest. The chance for truthful interchange dries up like a mud puddle in August.

Intimate Relationships

There is another reason for building acceptance, affection, approval and other qualities of intimacy into your marriage and family. It is vital for your mental well-being and physical health. Intimate relationships are lifelines in a maddening world. Yet the whole subject is foreign to the way many of us were raised. I know because of my own experience.

I grew up with the ethic that big boys don't cry, don't ask for attention, don't feel, don't hurt and never say never.

They just charge into action. The only acceptable emotion was anger, which you could display on the football field or basketball court. You could smack someone in the heat of battle. But if you got injured, you never admitted you felt pain. This is not unusual. Most guys around me grew up with a similar ethic.

It was a challenge to learn these principles, but a traumatic incident reinforced them. I still remember standing on the driveway of my home in Colorado Springs when Dad introduced me to the woman he said was going to be my new mother. My mother had endured numerous struggles. She spent time in a mental institution—back then we called them "insane asylums"—after I found her in a pool of blood after her second suicide attempt.

> The day my father walked onto the driveway and said he wanted to introduce my new mother, I resolved never to hug him again or shed another tear as long as I lived.

Despite her problems, I loved her. And I didn't understand why I needed a new mother. Most of all, I didn't want anything to do with those creepy little kids that my father said were going to be my new brothers and sisters. On that day I vowed that I would never hug my father again, never shed another tear.

Earlier I talked about the close friend who died in my place in combat. Even though he took his last breath lying in my arms, I never cried about it. In Vietnam I lost almost every buddy I had in combat. I loaded broken, twisted bodies and burned flesh on helicopters and never shed a tear. This pattern continued when I rejoined civilian life and married. I never let Susy see the inside.

However, after becoming a Christian, I learned that Jesus—the strongest man who ever lived—wept. I saw that I had real needs. And that the partner God had given me could help meet those needs. I'll never forget the first time I sat down with her and poured out my heart. Instead of bellowing out in anger, frustration and resentment, I said, "Honey, I really hurt. I've had a bad day." She nurtured me and held my head while I enjoyed a good cry.

There is nothing like freeing up our emotions the way Christ did, the way God designed us to do. He created us with emotions and the means to express them. I needed to learn how to do that. I'm thankful for a wife who has become very sensitive to some of my experiences.

A few years ago we traveled overseas to Asia. As we drove past a range of rice paddies in South Korea, it stirred some vivid memories. When you get ambushed in a rice paddy and lose a third of the men alongside you, you never forget it.

Rice paddies are unique. They're like flooded fields with rice sprouting up in the midst of the water. When I looked at them, in a flash of time I envisioned our troops charging across the muck in Vietnam. I could almost see the enemy troops dug in on the tree line. And feel the barbed wire they had strung along the dikes. Just like that, the ambush came springing back to life.

Staring out the car window, I whispered softly, "Wow."

Just then Susy leaned over and asked, "Phil, does this look like Vietnam?"

"Yeah, it does. It really does."

"Tell us a little bit about it," she said.

"Well, this is the way the rice paddies were over there . . ." I began. She and our children had heard the story before, and I didn't break into tears. But their willingness to listen was like a recognition of something I had been through. It represented a tender invitation to share something deep in my heart. One reason it meant so much is that when I returned from Vietnam, I couldn't share things with people. The war was unpopular and they didn't want to discuss it.

It was wonderful to have a wife who has been willing to say on certain occasions, "How did that feel? Would you just share with us?" I've been able to shed tears with the one whom God gave me as my helpmate, the one I love and need. I've been able to express my emotions the way the Lord Jesus did. Our children have also played a valuable role in listening to my old war stories and escapades, affirming me as a father and a man.

Letting these feelings out is not all teary-eyed stuff, either. I know the joy of sharing laughter and moments of hilarity with our family. This has been part of the Lord's plan to bring healing to my life from my dysfunctional, broken home and past war experiences. Whatever you have endured, creating intimate relationships in which you can express your deepest feelings will help repair the damage.

Working through Emotions

We have worked with our children to help them resolve problems with their intimate needs, not just in intra-family relationships, but as it affects their maturing into responsible adults. At a family conference once, they talked about some of the things they have learned about emotions. I think it is worth including a few of their comments. They show that building a team doesn't come easily. But the results of a close-knit, well-adjusted family will create eternal impact.

Anna: A few years ago I didn't feel secure enough to express my feelings to other people. When others jumped in and said something, then I would just clam up. Dad explained to me that people did want to hear what I had to say and that I shouldn't be quiet. Now it's a lot easier for me to tell others what I think and what I'm feeling. Dad really helped me with that.

> Helping children understand the differences they have with their brothers and sisters will prepare them for the time when they face differences with their spouse.

Abigail: Well, as much as I love Anna, we are very different—like night and day in many areas. That can cause a lot of strife as we argue over the way things should be done. I had to learn that just because she doesn't do something the way I would, that doesn't make my way right and her way wrong. That was hard for me to understand, but I'm thankful I have learned that. I realize how much I hurt her by not accepting her. I also see now how important it is for a younger sister to feel the acceptance and love of her older sister.

Joshua: I've struggled with my temper. Sometimes I take things out on Matt, Anna or even Paul, even though he's much bigger. Some of the verses Mom and Dad have given me come out of Ephesians. Like chapter 4, verse 26, which says that you can be angry and yet not sin. Nor should we let the day pass without letting go of that anger, because it gives the devil an opportunity to cause trouble.

I need to understand that if I let the day pass and I'm still mad at my brothers, that can grow into bitterness. That gives the devil a chance to stir things up. That passage goes on to say not to let an unwholesome word proceed from our mouths, but only what is edifying, so it will impart grace to those who hear. What that means to me is that I need to avoid saying things that don't lift others up, so my speech will give grace and encouragement to others.

Matthew: Ever since I was young, Dad told me if I didn't overcome my problem with my energetic little brother's teasing and nagging, I wouldn't be able to get ahold of my temper when I was older. He said if I couldn't get along with my brothers and sisters who are pretty much like me, then I wouldn't be able to get along with my spouse.

I knew he was right, but I had never seen any real-life examples. Then we met a young couple who were always being sarcastic and cutting each other down behind the other's back. They didn't hide their meanness. We felt embarrassed to be around them because they constantly fussed and argued with each other.

That was an incentive to change. I saw it was a good thing to control myself and put others first. I don't want to have that kind of marriage as an adult. So many people are getting divorced for petty reasons, things they can't even explain. It's like the fights I had with my brothers but then couldn't explain the reasons to our parents. I'm grateful for their good advice.

Paul: Several years ago, Matthew, Joshua and I were living in the same room. We are all very different. We had problems communicating and trying to decide things like,

"What should we do with the wet towel that's been sitting in the hallway for two days? Who put it there? What can we do to ensure that it doesn't happen again?" We worked hard on issues like that.

But we struggled with a major problem. I decided I was right and they were just being stubborn. They wouldn't listen or change. But that blinded me to their gifts. So I became overly critical and overreacted to minor irritations. The situations became like a series of open wounds that never healed.

This reminds me of when David came to his brothers who were camped with King Saul against the Philistines. As soon as his older brother heard him questioning some soldiers about Goliath, he became furious with him. He asked who was tending the sheep their father had entrusted to them. He accused him of being full of guile and wickedness and just coming to watch the battle.

Of course, God chose David to lead Israel and to be prominent in Christ's lineage. The Lord used this young, insignificant brother. As I worked through my resentment toward Matthew and Joshua and learned more about Scripture, I saw how we need to have the kind of heart that God will use. Since the Lord has given each of us gifts, I need to avoid stifling my brothers'. They need to learn to be leaders. I need to let them thrive so the Lord can use them in a great and mighty way.

Questions for Reflection

1. Ask your spouse to rate you on each of the principles of intimacy. Be sure to say (for example), "How does acceptance look to you?" Discuss the differences in your ratings and what you might do to improve.

2. Now ask your children to rate you. Make notes of what you need to change.

3. If your children argue and pick at each other, how might they be learning that behavior from you and your spouse? What steps can you take to help them appreciate each other's differences and grow closer?

4. How do your children express their thoughts and fears to you? If they don't feel free to do that, what steps can you take to help them feel willing to share?

5. When is the last time you sat and talked with your family? Sit down and tell them about some of the hardships, trials and disappointments you felt growing up. Ask God to free you up to show the emotions you are feeling.

Note

1. From *Unlimited Partnership: Building Intimacy and Teamwork into Your Marriage* by Phil and Susy Downer and David and Theresa Ferguson. Intimacy Press, Austin, Texas, 1996.

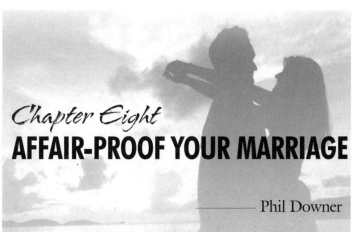

Chapter Eight
AFFAIR-PROOF YOUR MARRIAGE

———— Phil Downer

I'll never forget the scene in Hawaii. As we sat on the edge of a beach on the island of Maui, I marveled at the breathtaking view near our cabana. If there were a prettier picture of the ocean, I had never seen it. No painting could fully capture the richness or texture of fluffy clouds, a deep azure sky and another island in the distance.

Suddenly I glanced over and saw a group of bikini-clad women lounging on beach chairs shaded by umbrellas. Whoa.

Gazing out on the ocean, Susy said, "Look at that."

"Yeah, look at that," I echoed, my gaze diverted.

"Isn't that beautiful?"

Yeah, I thought. *Too beautiful.*

It was a bit unbelievable. Our eyes were taking in two completely different pictures. She couldn't see what had grabbed my attention. And so it is with many women. They sometimes fail to comprehend—or least appreciate—what men experience.

As we walk through a stadium filled with 50,000 people at a ball game, our eyes scan curves, blondes and scantily attired females. That doesn't take much effort. What takes effort is to avoid staring. Just as women smell, hear and sense things that we are oblivious to, men see differently.

To deny this is to deny gravity or that the sun rises in the east. God made us with natural physical urges. For a long time I made excuses and felt silent guilt for the way God made me. But today I feel more of an urgency to discuss reality. We are living in too dangerous a time to stick our heads in the sand any longer.

Sometimes it almost seems like a cruel joke. Why would God give men such a strong appetite when He knew it would be so hard to control? I think one reason is so we could develop a sensitivity for our weakness. It takes a life wrapped around Jesus Christ just to make it through the day. Some days are harder than others. When men fall to temptation, they aren't necessarily evil or purely self-centered. Some never develop the tools to withstand it.

> "I have made a covenant with my eyes;
> how then could I gaze at a virgin?"
> —Job 31:1

I'm convinced this is not an area we can fully understand. But this much I am sure of: I don't believe many women understand the pressure and attraction the female figure has for men. That includes godly husbands who strive to remain committed to their marriage and devoted to their wives. I tried once to explain this to Susy and our daughters, Abigail and Anna, and they gave me a funny look, as if to say, "You've got to be kidding."

I realize that plenty of women give men the eye too. But I still believe that God wired men a bit differently. If some women could climb inside a man's head and see what he sees, hear what he hears and understand what he thinks when a good-looking woman walks by, they would be shocked.

I have heard countless numbers of women say, "If my husband ever looked at another woman, I don't know what I would do." They better start wondering. It isn't a question of whether a man is going to look. It's question of what he will do during the millisecond after he looks. We men must learn to guard our hearts. Like Job, we have to make a covenant to turn our eyes away and shut down our wandering imaginations.

Wives, you play a key role in helping your mate avoid temptation. Don't be like the Christian friend whose wife asked him to accompany her to a Victoria's Secret outlet. I later told him, "You're lying to your wife."

> "You have heard that it was said, 'YOU SHALL NOT COMMIT ADULTERY'; but I say to you that everyone who looks on a woman with lust for her has already committed adultery with her in his heart."
> —Matthew 5:27-28

"What do you mean?"

"You're lying to your wife if you think you can go into a store like that and not tell her what's going through your mind. Does she think you can go into a store like that and keep thoughts that are pure and affectionate for her?"

His downcast eyes and silence spoke loudly.

Women often don't take such matters seriously. It happened in our home. One time Susy had a Victoria's Secret catalog lying around the house. Like millions, her name found its way onto a mailing list. Before becoming a Christian, I spent good money on *Playboy* magazines to see pictures like that. That stuff is lethal; it will rot the inside of your heart. I told her, "You can't let this stuff come into the house."

"Oh, OK, honey." She shrugged absent-mindedly. "I'll take care of it."

Soon another catalog showed up in the mail. I repeated my warning, reminding her we had young males in our house who were quickly maturing.

"Oh, OK," she smiled. But I could tell she didn't understand. To her it was just underwear. Who would want to look at some stranger? One time she had said, "Body parts are all the same."

Sure enough, a third one came. I decided it was time to act.

"Wow, Susy, look at this thing," I said, waving it in the air. "Whoa, look at this babe. She must be about nineteen."

"Give me that," my wife replied, grabbing it out of my hand as she burst into tears. Marching to the nearest phone, she called a toll-free number and ordered her name promptly removed from their mailing list.

How Men Are Wired

It may sound silly to worry about lingerie catalogs when we face a daily deluge of pornography via the Internet, cable television and the corner newsstand, but it all matters. Whatever we take in through our senses can work its way down into our heart and lead to disaster. Vigilance in every area is a must if we are to affair-proof our marriages.

This applies to husbands as well as wives. We must guard each other's hearts daily and take steps to ensure that we reserve our affections and attentions solely for our mate. But I like to especially warn women that they are living with the biggest fools on earth when it comes to the opposite sex. We are as dumb as trees when it comes to avoiding the lure of the female figure.

How many men have given up empires for some woman they barely knew? Look at David, the king of Israel and one of the most powerful men on the face of the earth in his time. Did he know anything about Bathsheba? Did he know if she were going to make a great mother? Had he tasted her pot roast and figured she could cook up a feast every night? No, he only knew how she looked. He put his whole kingdom on the line, along with his generation, his children and his relationship with the Lord. And he fell.

If he can do that, I can do that. I'm not stronger than the king who slaughtered the Philistines. Evidence abounds that millions are susceptible. One evangelical denomination recently announced a program to help its pastors, since an estimated twenty percent of all ministers are involved in pornography and sexual addiction.[1]

How can this be? Simple. Visual attraction. It gets a man every time. To draw a parallel, when our oldest daughter was about twelve, I wanted to explain the makeup of men in a way she could understand. I wanted to discuss the facts of life with her honestly and tell her the truth about the pull of sex. So I used our dogs as an example.

At the time, we had two young, good-sized female dogs and a male who was even bigger. Pointing at Prince, I asked Abigail about him. After bantering back and forth about Prince and what a great dog he was, I asked what we did with the dogs when the females were in heat.

"Well, we take them off to the vet and kennel them because they're too young to have pups," she replied. "We keep them in the kennel until they calm down."

"Well, what happens when we bring one of them back and she still has that scent, even though she's out of heat? Does Prince go a little crazy? What does he do?"

"Oh, Dad, it is so disgusting," she frowned. "I don't even want to talk about it."

"Yeah," chimed in Susy, "and we're not going to talk about it."

"Yes, we are," I persisted. "What does Prince do?"

> "For it would be better for them not to have known the way of righteousness, than having known it, to turn away from the holy commandment handed on to them. It has happened to them according to the true proverb, 'A DOG RETURNS TO ITS OWN VOMIT,' and, 'A sow, after washing, returns to wallowing in the mire.'"
> —2 Peter 2:21-22

"Dad," Abigail whined, "I don't want to talk about it."

"You're twelve years old, you're learning a lot now and you're growing up," I pressed. "Where does he put his nose?"

No matter how distasteful this discussion, I kept at it to make a point. Finally, I asked what happened when we brought back the second female after she was out of heat.

"Well, then he just does the same thing with her. It's the most disgusting thing."

"That's right," I said. "Let me tell you, Abigail, if you attract a man by the way you look, that's just about how long he will last. He'll stick around until the next good-looking female comes by. God gave dogs this attraction to scent, but what did he give men?"

She and Susy shrugged, curious looks on their faces.

"Visual attraction. We can't control the urge to look much better than we can stop a dog from reacting to scents," I said. "That is, the initial attraction. We are attracted to those shapes. What we do with it after we're attracted to it is our decision. That's why we need your help to avoid things."

> "If your eye causes you to stumble, throw it out; it is better for you to enter the kingdom of God with one eye, than, having two eyes, to be cast into hell, where THEIR WORM DOES NOT DIE, AND THE FIRE IS NOT QUENCHED."
> —Mark 9:47-48

Men, you need to get honest with your wives and daughters. Don't pretend you don't have normal male hormones. One time, as the family was gathered around, I asked our sons (who were then all under twelve) if they liked watching the Olympics the night before on television. They all nodded enthusiastically, particularly when I asked if they liked the figure skating.

"What did you watch during the figure skating?"

"Well, what do you mean, Dad?"

"Did you watch the men or the women?"

"Oh, we watched the women."

"What part of the women did you look at it? Did you watch the women's legs as they were skating around in those itty-bitty skirts?"

They all nodded as Susy and the girls' mouths hung open. They couldn't believe it. But it was true.

Dressing the Part

Abigail took my lesson to heart. The next summer we were at the Olympics in person, thanks to a friend who found us some great tickets in Atlanta. Seated right in front of us was a woman wearing a cutoff, sleeveless blouse—a skimpy garment that looked like a shrunken T-shirt. When she pulled back her arms, you could say the whole world was on display.

Seeing the distraction, Abigail leaned forward, tapped her on the shoulder and said, "Excuse me. When you sit like that you can see right into your chest. That is really distracting for my father and my brothers. Would you mind turning yourself around?"

Of course, sometimes she needs feedback too. Like the time she came down from her room dressed in a snazzy, modern-looking outfit—a real eye-catching, low-cut number that blinked like a neon sign. When she asked what I thought, I said, "Abigail, I'll tell you what. The girls see you and they're going to like it. They'll think it's fashionable. But do you know what the guys are going to look at with you wearing that?"

"Uh, I'll go change," she said.

This may sound too basic, but I think we need a return to basics. Our culture has sunk to such low levels that we can easily be lulled to sleep, thinking we're doing fine because we don't look so bad compared to the world. But that's the wrong standard to embrace. We need to look at God's standards.

Comparing ourselves to the world leads to the kind of situation I encountered on a business-related trip to another city. During the weekend I spoke to a Sunday school class at one of the area's most prestigious churches. The leader was a member of the local affiliate of a national Christian organization. Just as I was getting ready to speak, his wife walked in wearing a dress that had men's eyes popping out and sat down in the front row.

During my presentation, I talked about some of the issues of dress and purity. It tickled me when, about halfway through my talk, she leaned over and asked her husband for his blazer so she could cover herself up. Sometimes that's what we need to do—cover ourselves up. We don't need to put on a show for the world.

> "No temptation has overtaken you
> but such as is common to man;
> and God is faithful, who will not
> allow you to be tempted beyond what
> you are able, but with the temptation
> will provide the way of escape also, so
> that you will be able to endure it."
> —1 Corinthians 10:13

I challenge wives to make a covenant with God that they would not present themselves in such a way that they intend to attract the looks of other men. Pray as you go through your closet and ask God if there are things in there that you shouldn't be wearing. When you get up in the morning, ask yourself if you are putting on clothes so somebody else other than your husband will notice you.

Husbands, do the same. Are you primping in the mirror each morning and carefully selecting outfits that you hope will attract female gazes? Do you engage in water-cooler talk that gets dangerously close to serious flirtation? If your wife were standing next to you in such situations, would she get upset?

If you're chuckling over what a prude I am, let me point out that the mildly suggestive dress or handsome suit that leads to the innocent lunch that leads to the innocent meeting after work that winds up in a full-blown affair has destroyed millions of marriages.

> "Therefore consider the members of your earthly body as dead to immorality, impurity, passion, evil desire, and greed, which amounts to idolatry. . . .
> But now you also, put them all aside: anger, wrath, malice, slander, and abusive speech from your mouth."
> —Colossians 3:5, 8

We live in a time when Satan is working feverishly to destroy couples. He hates your guts. He hates your purity. He hates your attractiveness to your mate. He will do anything to rot you on the inside so that you'll blow up on the outside. And all the while he whispers, "It won't matter if you dress that way. Look at what everyone else has on. Do you want to be considered odd?"

Instead of following the world and looking like the world, we need to remember the advice of Colossians 3. God wants us to put to death immorality, impurity, passion, evil desire, greed and idolatry. He wants us to put aside anger, wrath, malice, slander and abusive speech. I call them the "dirty dozen." We need to walk away from them and never look back.

For me, that meant putting to death the tendency to flirt with disaster. In the past I would check into a hotel and see the magazines or cable guides they had lying on the desk. I wouldn't watch the racy programs, but I would read the titles and imagine what might be in those movies. Finally I got into the habit of taking those publications and stuffing them in the drawer where I couldn't see them.

Even then, there are never-ending temptations to open the drawer, particularly in cyberspace. Like the friend of mine who got involved in adultery through the Internet, a common tale of the twenty-first century. Though a godly man, one night he visited a site with various chat rooms and started chatting with a woman. Over time he found himself staying up late and getting up early to continue their conversations.

He never intended for it to happen. But over time he was running to the computer to see if there was another message. One day this stranger showed up at his home. She flew clear across the country and landed on his doorstep. What he did had already been determined by months of previous contact. He already made that decision because a seed planted in his mind blossomed in his heart.

I'm not making any excuses for his behavior because he is a friend. He could have stopped months before by recognizing it and turning away from the computer. But by the time the temptation stood in front of his eyes, he was unable to resist. Too many people scoff at the notion that dipping their toe in the ocean could eventually drown them.

Keep the Home Fires Burning

One time a "lady of the evening" approached me as I was on my way to a court hearing at about 10 o'clock in the morning. After she made her offer, I replied, "Jesus will forgive you." She stood there, a stunned look on her face. But I didn't linger for any extended conversation. I knew hanging around too long could spell trouble.

Another occasion proved easier to resist, since Abigail was seated next to me and Susy was on the same bus. We were going to a faraway terminal after an overseas flight on a mission trip. Suddenly a stewardess—I later learned she was the airline's lead flight attendant—smiled and suggested, "How would you like to buy me a drink back at the hotel?" Abigail sat there with her mouth hanging open. When Susy heard about it, she said, "I don't think she was thirsty."

> "The one who commits adultery with a woman is lacking sense; he who would destroy himself does it. Wounds and disgrace he will find, and his reproach will not be blotted out."
> —Proverbs 6:32-33

Temptation isn't always so blatant. But everyone who goes into an office, factory, school or other workplace knows how easily it can crop up. One time a woman propositioned me in the office. Shaking my head, I said, "No, thank you, I give at home."

One sure way to avoid trouble is to decide ahead of time what you will say. Make a vow that should someone from the opposite sex give you a subtle look, graze your leg or ask you to lunch, you will either say no or walk away without saying anything. Making a firm decision in advance will prevent waffling and indecision later.

The same applies to meals out when you're traveling alone. Fast-food restaurants are fine with me. The food at Hardee's or McDonald's won't kill you and you'll find far fewer temptations than at those trendy clubs or rock-n-roll palaces. Even at common diners, I pray a lot when I'm alone. Many people don't like solitude. They're afraid of things the Lord might point out to them. But this is a great opportunity to practice the presence of God.

Remember the story in chapter 1 about the Malaysian airline attendant who approached me? I still know her room number: 905. After I told Susy, she asked why I remembered. "Sorry," I told her, "but I can't forget it. It's stuck in my mind as a token of how easily I can face situations where I am susceptible."

Susy didn't appreciate that at first. But she did like my calling to tell her about it. Why would I do such a thing? Because I believe in including my wife among my accountability partners. And as soon as I tell my accountability partners about a situation, it serves as an automatic check against reconsidering a decision.

I've known men who said "no" but then mulled the offer over. Entertained it. Meditated on it. Thought about maybe just having a little conversation; after all, they were lonely. And sure enough, they wound up caving in to their imagination. A little talk led much further.

Another reason I told Susy about this flight attendant is that I consider her to be my best friend. Best friends don't keep secrets from each other. If we're going to live together for the rest of our lives, then we want to stoke the fires of excitement and appreciation. Sharing close thoughts and concern is how deep, intimate friendships are built.

Husbands, pledge to make a covenant with the Lord that your wife will be the most precious, wonderful person in your life. Treat your mate like the source of joy that she should be. Make her your only source of physical fulfillment. A woman needs to know she is special, and if she is your only physical outlet she will feel special.

> "With her many persuasions she entices him; with her flattering lips she seduces him. Suddenly he follows her as an ox goes to the slaughter, or as one in fetters to the discipline of a fool, until an arrow pierces through his liver; as a bird hastens to the snare, so he does not know that it will cost him his life."
> —Proverbs 7:21-23

Even after three decades together, Susy and I have a joyous physical relationship. But it takes a commitment and a focus. Sure, it's a challenge. Everything worthwhile takes effort. However, I believe God places a need in humans for loyalty, fidelity and faithfulness. Only when we listen to Satan do we get deceived and drawn off the path.

I know I've spent a lot of time talking about the lure females have for men. But husbands, don't get complacent. With the majority of women now in the workplace, they face a barrage of temptation too. Offices are filled with divorced men or those who think nothing of a "fling."

Don't get deceived thinking that women all over the country are leaving home for the muscle-bound movie star types or the brilliant Ph.Ds. You know who attracts the most attention? Men who treat wives nice at work. They're kind and gentle, the type of man most women crave. They may be putting on the biggest act around and may be the biggest liars on the face of the earth, but every day wives fall for it and throw their marriages away.

A Wife's View

Susy Downer

For a long time, when I heard about husbands who had strayed from their marriage, I focused on the men's mistakes and weaknesses. But after years of Phil's sharing openly with me (as I shared in chapter 6), I realized Christian wives have a lot more responsibility in this area than many of us like to admit. God has made us a team. We need to take responsibility for the part that God has given to us. As best we can, we need to protect our husbands from falling into temptation.

Women, this may be difficult to discuss. It was for me. My parents never talked about their physical relationship. They modeled deep love and commitment to us and have a wonderful marriage. But they weren't comfortable telling me about the physical aspect of marriage. Not surprisingly, I was totally unprepared for its importance to Phil.

It was his number one priority and often it didn't even make my list. That's a pretty serious difference. Now, I never remember refusing Phil, but there is a big difference between saying "no" (which I didn't do) and being a loving, encouraging, enthusiastic partner. I was never the initiator, showing deep love for Phil.

Early in our marriage, he would remark, "I just love you more than you love me." And I would think, *Why does he say that?* I began to realize part of it was because I never made a move toward him. That was his priority, his department. I never really said this or even thought much about it, but looking back, I know that was my perspective.

Because this was such a difficult part of our marriage, Phil would often bring up the subject and want to talk to me about it. You may be able to imagine my reaction. I would get flushed, feel heat rising from my cheeks and declare, "I don't want to talk about it." That would frustrate and upset him, but it was too uncomfortable for me. It's still not a subject I tackle with ease.

But when the Lord began mending our marriage, I felt a deep desire to improve. That, coupled with conferences where the subject would periodically be discussed, made me think that I needed to push myself out of my comfort zone and at least be willing to talk about it. That was my first mini-step. Actually, it wasn't talking. I just promised to listen without getting judgmental or upset.

Knowing how hard that was for me, Phil showed his appreciation for this move. In the beginning, I wasn't prepared to hear the truth about his feelings. Time after time, I came away flabbergasted. When you have never heard any frank discussion on the subject, it is a total shock. And as liberated as people like to think they are and as worldly as they pretend to be, many have never sat through such discussions.

As I mentioned earlier, there are women available for our husbands everywhere they go. Over the years, Phil has struggled with having secretaries who are overly attractive; on other occasions, hotel concierges have thrown themselves at him. He needed to talk about the problems this caused him. As I became more willing to listen and encouraged him to share, he became more open.

> "The wife does not have authority over her own body, but the husband does; and likewise also the husband does not have authority over his own body, but the wife does."
> —1 Corinthians 7:4

When we first started talking about such issues, I remember thinking, *Now, don't react. Don't say something negative. Don't say the wrong thing.* While I appreciated his honesty, it was also making me nervous. I wasn't sure what to say, so I wouldn't say anything.

That would in turn make Phil nervous and he would finally ask, "Well, what do you think?"

"What do you mean?"

"Well, I need some feedback," he would say. "Are you mad at me or what?"

I realized not saying anything was sending the wrong message. He was stretching himself just to honestly share with me, so my not responding or saying much about it felt

terribly discouraging to him. I had to learn to say, "Phil,
thank you for being this honest with me. I will pray for
you." Then I needed to be faithful to do that.

When he said that men need their wives to hold them accountable, I saw that I needed to go back later and say,
"Phil, how are you doing with that secretary?" or "Have
any more problems with any concierges?" Believe it or not,
he appreciated that.

> "Love is patient, love is kind and is not
> jealous; love does not brag and is not
> arrogant, does not act unbecomingly;
> it does not seek its own, is not
> provoked, does not take into account a
> wrong suffered, does not rejoice in
> unrighteousness, but rejoices with the
> truth; bears all things, believes all things,
> hopes all things, endures all things."
> —1 Corinthians 13:4-7

Wives, if your husband will go so far as to reveal his inner
feelings and share such a personal part of his psyche, be careful not to jump on him. I've had women tell me that the first
time their husband said something like this they shot back,
"You have a lot of nerve to do that." Can you imagine that
husband was ever going to come back and share honestly
with his wife? Very unlikely.

We need to be praying for our husbands, encouraging and
supporting them. It takes a lot of effort to recognize and change
our ways of thinking. Earlier in this book, Phil mentioned the

Victoria's Secret catalog. That wasn't the only time. On another occasion he asked me to pull the Sears and Penney's catalogs out of the mail. He said if I wanted to keep them, I needed to put them where he and the boys wouldn't see them.

By the look on my face when he said that, I know he could tell I was thinking, *This isn't natural. The Penney's and the Sears catalogs?* Because my heart wasn't in it, I wasn't too faithful to pay attention to his request.

Then one summer I was at a homeschool conference and I ate lunch alone one day. Down the table a ways, I overheard two men talking to each other, discussing this very subject. This man was telling his friend exactly what Phil had said about the importance of keeping those catalogs away from yourself—and especially adolescent and teenage boys.

As he talked about how important that was, my face took on a crimson hue. When a man I didn't know or had any reason to respect said the same thing as my husband, it lent credibility to what Phil had said. I had to go home and confess, "I am so sorry that I haven't respected you in this area. I haven't been obedient or realized that God gave you wisdom to protect our family. I am so sorry."

To those wives who have husbands who want to be faithful and focus on us with their love and attention, be extremely grateful for that. Do your part to keep your marriages exciting. Strive to be so loving and enthusiastic about your husband that he will never have the desire to go anywhere else but home to you.

Questions for Reflection

If these questions are too sensitive for group discussion, pair off with your mate or a close friend of the same sex to discuss them.

1. What was your first exposure to the allure of the opposite sex? How did that affect your outlook on marriage?
2. What three things can you do to make yourself attractive to your mate?
3. Name three steps you can take to avoid exposing yourself to temptation at the office or when you are traveling on business.
4. Name three qualities of your mate that excite you.
5. Describe the state of your marriage. What is good about it? How could it become better?
6. Women, what do you think about Susy's comment that early in marriage she never initiated physical contact? Should women take this step? Why or why not?
7. Men, have you been honest with your wife about your needs and struggles? How could you improve communication with her in this area?

Note

1. "Assemblies of God Tackles Problem of Porn Addiction Among Ministers," *Charisma*, January 2001, p. 24.

Chapter Nine
THINGS THAT LAST

———— Phil Downer

How much is enough? We have a hard time answering that question. In America, where citizens live in the kind of luxury ninety percent of the world only dreams about, millions treat a never-ending series of toys as necessities. In First Timothy 6, Paul said we are to be content if we have food, shelter and clothing. Cable TV, multiple phone lines, pagers, laptop computers, BMWs, hot tubs and cruise control don't qualify.

I remember the time I met a couple in New York. A Christian business owner, the husband had become a multimillionaire at the age of thirty-three. Despite a business valued at $7 million, he was preparing to acquire a competitor and triple his company's sales volume. Concerned about the demands that would place on his time and its effect on his young family, I tried to caution him.

"Why are you doing this?"

"I just wanted to give more money to the Lord," he replied.

That's a lie, I thought. "Tell me, what do you do with your free time?"

155

He told of enjoying working in a lay ministry and discipling a couple of men. But I grew suspicious when he
added, "and some other things."

"You have $7 million," I said. "That could free up a lot of
time to disciple guys."

"No, I'm really too busy to take on anything else."

"Well, let me ask you this," I said. "Is this acquisition going to give you more time with your family?"

"No."

"Let me ask again: Why are you doing this?"

> "I know how to get along with humble
> means, and I also know how to live in
> prosperity; in any and every circumstance
> I have learned the secret of being filled
> and going hungry, both of having
> abundance and suffering need."
> —Philippians 4:12

"Well, I just want to take the opportunity. It's an investment, you know. Sort of like the parable of the talents and
all of that."

Sensing something lay behind his insatiable drive for
more, I said, "Tell me about your father."

"My what?" he said, his eyebrows raising.

"Your father."

He paused, a strange look crossing his face. I had
touched a nerve.

"Well . . . I hate him."

"What does he do for a living?"

"He has another business across town," the man said, a mixture of regret and anger showing on his face. "He cut me out of the business. I'll never get one dime out of it."

"So you're working to prove your self-worth to your father."

"No, I'm not," he shook his head.

"Well, let's just kind of dig around here. What is your impression of God? You know we get our impression of God from our impression of our father."

That touched off a long discussion. Finally his wife jumped in and pointed the finger. "Yes, you are working to prove yourself to Dad," she said and rolled on fast and furious with examples. She scolded him for his vain efforts that were reaping unhappiness in their home.

Unless he corrected the situation, major trouble lay ahead. In his craving to work so hard to prove his value, this Christian businessman was driving toward divorce court. The question he had to ask himself was: What good is a fortune if you don't have a family to share life with?

It's the same question we all must ask ourselves. Why are we working? What are our priorities? What are we doing instead of investing in the lives of other people? What things do you think you can buy that will feed the hunger in your soul for deep, long-lasting relationships?

I remember the gold watch I used to own. It had a gold chain and a hunter-style case—a thing of real beauty. I bought it when we were in England, before I became a Christian. When I spotted it, I thought, *Boy, if I had that watch, I would never be sad again.*

Guess what? It kept me satisfied for about twenty-four hours. You can't hug a watch. Nor a car, a house, a computer, a fifty-two-inch projection television or seats at the opera. None of them can hug you back. Things can't feed your inner self. Given this reality, do you want to invest in a six-figure IRA or what will last for eternity?

Fruit That Lasts

For years I was the first guy in the office and the last one to leave. You might think when I was an attorney that I focused solely on the courtroom. Not true. Being part of a multi-office law firm includes a lot of business. I'm a businessman through and through. I love it. I love going to people's offices and scanning the pictures on their walls. It's like getting a bird's-eye view of their life.

But when I became a Christian, life changed. Not overnight; it took years to deal with the long list of flaws and shortcomings that had become treasured habits. Giving up my security and pride in my own efforts proved to be a major adjustment. I had to learn to trust that the Lord would supply all of our needs. The lesson continued when I became president of a ministry that touched lives around the nation.

Part of that trust involved setting aside the drive to get to the office first every morning. What a hard habit to give up! But I wasn't giving it up so I could sleep later. I used those early morning hours to spend time with God in prayer, Bible study and in discipling our children. Suddenly I found myself hitting the parking lot around 9 o'clock. That wasn't easy. Seven years into changing my routine, I would pull up and go, "Oh, man, everyone's going to get ahead of me. I'm behind on so many things. What have I been thinking?"

I constantly fought battles with fear—fear of others getting ahead of me, not pulling my own weight or maybe losing my job. This is where trust becomes so valuable. We live in a society where overtime and pushing everyone to the limit is accepted business practice. Resisting the pull of "more, more, more" is harder than ever. That is why it helps to stop regularly and ask ourselves, "What am I working for?"

Investing is more than the rate of return on your mutual fund. Far more. Fifty years from now nobody will remember how much money you earned. But if you train your children in righteousness and teach them God's Word, and they in turn disciple their children, who do the same for their children, your impact will literally continue for eternity.

> "Do not store up for yourselves treasures on earth, where moth and rust destroy, and where thieves break in and steal. But store up for yourselves treasures in heaven, where neither moth nor rust destroys, and where thieves do not break in or steal; for where your treasure is, there your heart will be also."
> —Matthew 6:19-21

What treasures are you leaving for the next generation? Are you toiling day and night to leave behind piles of cash that will likely be spent in a few years? Automobiles, finances, insurance policies, jobs, public recognition, civic awards and all the other things that people strive for . . . are all headed for the scrap heap of history. Sooner rather than later.

The things that last are simple: God's Word and His children. The people that we invest in and minister to will leave the kind of lasting imprint that we want to make. This starts with our natural children and extends to our spiritual children. They will live on as fruit that lasts. This is investing for eternity instead of momentary satisfaction.

As humans, we tend to see so little beyond our life span. We think of the next few years instead of the next few centuries. Even Christians make that mistake. Yet if we believe we're going to live forever with the One who rules the universe and holds it together, shouldn't we listen to what He tells us? In Matthew 28:19, Christ instructed us to go into all the world and make disciples, not converts, not members of our church, nor wholehearted backers of our favorite organization.

> Years from now, your children won't remember what they got for Christmas or how many steak dinners they ate. What they will remember is how much time you spent with them, what lessons you taught them about life and the insights you showed them from the Bible.

In other words, He was telling us to pour our lives into people. Disciple your children at home. Disciple others in the community. Be like the man I know in California who came to Christ in his sixties. He had a lot of mistakes to overcome at that age, but he didn't agonize over his failures. He devoted the next twenty years to making disciples. He went back to his kids and reconciled his differences with them and taught them well. He talked to family and his neighbors.

Today there are young men and women and married couples up and down the West Coast who owe their solid standing in life to this man's influence. He discipled men half his age. It was absolutely amazing to see what that man accomplished in the latter part of his life. He finished well and made a difference. His impact won't fully unfold for years to come. He left behind treasures that will last.

Setting Priorities

Tell me what you're afraid of and I'll tell you your priorities. If you grew up with a fear of losing money and not having a lot of money, you probably spend too much time worrying about your money instead of your children. If you grew up without many friends, you may be striving to be "the hostess with the mostest."

> "So then, none of you can be My disciple who does not give up all his own possessions. Therefore, salt is good; but if even salt has become tasteless, with what will it be seasoned?"
> —Luke 14:33-34

A big problem with trying to compensate for your past is that you are planting the same seeds in your children. If you model your weakness for your children, they will embrace it and carry it on for years to come. That is why it is so important to continually take stock of yourself and what you are doing to pass on a legacy of value—morals, integrity, principles, honesty and faith in God. That is the kind of inheritance that won't decay.

Why can't you take one day a week and devote a healthy chunk of it to your children? Why can't you take one night a week and go out on a date with your spouse? Why can't you take one hour away from the television set to talk to your neighbors? Why can't you spend more time with friends to encourage them and lift their spirits?

I have a friend who worked all his life for the freedom of retirement. But when he made it, he invested it in more bondage: He started another business. Not because he needed the responsibilities or the cash—he had more than enough—but he wanted *just a little bit more*. This man had made disciples and been involved in ministry. He could have devoted even more time to those efforts. By pursuing the course he did, he later wound up entangled in a painful business-related mess.

By contrast, Jim Lyon, the man I first mentioned in chapter 5, has a focus on eternity. So does his wife, Mary Gail. For thirty years Jim has juggled a busy medical practice while his wife had her hands full raising four children. Yet each made a priority of "things that last" over those that don't. Jim turned down numerous opportunities to do things that would have benefited his medical practice so he could spend more time with his wife and family. He also made discipling men a priority.

When their children were living at home, Jim always made time to disciple one or two men, and Mary Gail one or two women. Once their children had grown up, Jim met with up to nine men a week while his wife met with eight. While many women return to work when the nest empties, Mary Gail felt called by God to help women be better wives, mothers and children of God. Early in their married and professional lives this couple made a conscious decision to forgo the riches of this world for the treasures of the next. Once a financial planner told Jim, "You are the poorest doctor of all my clients. I can't believe how little you make." Jim just laughed; he and Mary Gail are living for the things that last.

Like that misguided man who needed one more business, most of what we're investing in will burn up like a campfire. Why not invest in things that last forever? Namely, spiritual reproduction. It takes an investment of some things that everyone owns: time; yourself; father power or mother power; the ability to guide, encourage, exhort and influence.

> "The things which you have heard from me in the presence of many witnesses, entrust these to faithful men who will be able to teach others also."
> —2 Timothy 2:2

Devoting your exclusive attention to your child, for even an hour a week, is worth more than hundreds of hours your child may spend with a youth pastor, a school teacher or a soccer coach. That hour is far more valuable than sitting in the stands watching him or her run down the field. Friends have often told me, "Well, I go to all their games." That's important, going to the games. But that's not a relationship. You can miss a few games and still teach your child one-on-one. Tell your son you love him, care about him and are always going to stand behind him and that no matter what he does, you love him because God loves you that way.

Walk with your daughter and praise her for her beauty— especially the talents and abilities that are worth more than mere looks. Tell her how much you love her mother and are looking forward to living with her forever, as well as watching your daughter grow up.

The stock market explosion of the 1990s sidetracked too many people with the promise of fast money, and they lost the treasures that matter. That's why I've devoted a lot of time thus far in this chapter to discussing investments and priorities: They determine the direction the rest of your life will take.

> "We also exult in our tribulations, knowing that tribulation brings about perseverance; and perseverance, proven character; and proven character, hope; and hope does not disappoint."
> —Romans 5:3-5

In Second Timothy, Paul instructed Timothy to pass on the teachings he had heard to others. This is the principle of spiritual reproduction. The older generation teaches the younger, who teaches the generation coming after them. The payoff comes at the end of your life. This is demonstrated by two friends who offer a contrast between the value of discipling and the emptiness of activity.

The first man, named Chuck, was very wealthy. He managed a profitable factory. However, what mattered wasn't his money. It was how he spent the latter half of his life. Realizing what truly made a difference, he spent time discipling a few men a year, sometimes more, sometimes less. But he passed on his business acumen, his insights on life and confronting problems, and the Scriptures that had helped him thrive and withstand pressures.

When Chuck died, the church was packed. Besides his family and fellow church members, many of his spiritual sons and grandsons came. They wanted to pay their respects and praise the Lord for what He had done through this man. At the end, he had given what truly mattered—his life. Which is one of the most important points about Chuck. Initially he hadn't spent a lot of time with his children. He neglected the eternal for the temporary. But it wasn't too late to change.

I visited the other friend, who I'll call Randy, when he was on his deathbed from heart trouble. A Christian, he had filled his hours with public service and prestigious awards. But he never got down to the nitty-gritty of sharing openly with others for the purpose of training, instructing and encouraging them. As a result, he felt empty. I could see it in his eyes and hear it in his prayers.

Despite all his service, the ministries he served were going on without him. The church boards no longer needed him. Members who barely knew him beyond formal meetings never called. He wasn't a bad or neglectful father, but since he had failed to build much of a relationship with his children, they were moving on easily without him as well. He died in a lonely state, embittered over the lack of caring he felt in his dying hours.

Role Models

Discipleship is a tough task because it calls for acting as a role model. Part of that role includes transparency. Don't be afraid to reveal your past mistakes. We can help others overcome their problems by sharing what helped us correct our errors. That is how the man who first discipled me helped me take a major step toward Christian growth.

When Jim volunteered to meet with me once a week, I was still struggling. Yes, I had accepted Christ as my Savior, but I still had a lot of rough edges. I packed a lot of garbage and my temper bursts at home hadn't completely subsided.

One day, as we discussed investments, Jim opened up. A doctor, he was obviously embarrassed as he talked about losing a fortune on a deal that went sour. He was afraid I would laugh when he revealed that he had lost all his money. Despite those fears, he shared the episode and what he had learned from it.

> "No temptation has overtaken you but such as is common to man; and God is faithful, who will not allow you to be tempted beyond what you are able, but with the temptation will provide the way of escape also, so that you will be able to endure it."
> —1 Corinthians 10:13

My first thought when he told me about the investment was, *Stupid doctor, lost all his money.* Yet because of his willingness to be transparent, I learned the lesson from Romans, how suffering produces endurance, and endurance, character. From character comes hope, which doesn't disappoint us.

Years later I had a chance to pass on this lesson. At the time, I was discipling several men who were about twenty years younger than I. One of them told me he wanted some accountability. I replied, "OK, you be accountable to me and I'll be accountable to you. I want you to pray for me when I'm in a hotel room alone."

"Really?" he asked.

"Yeah. I don't want to turn on that television, with that pornography and the other stuff that's on cable. It is a temptation for me."

I could see this guy's bubble pop. All the air went out of the unrealistic image he held of me like a giant air balloon had imploded.

"You have a problem with that?" he repeated. "I can't believe that you would have a problem with that."

He didn't say it, but I could sense him silently thinking, *I've never had a problem with that.*

We didn't have much contact after that. About a year and a half later, he called. "When you told me about the struggle you had with stuff on television, I was really critical of you," he said. "I thought, 'Here you are the big-time ministry guy and you've got struggles with *that?*' Well, then I went to Houston. It was a tough week. My wife and I were not getting along real well, even though we have a great marriage. I turned that TV on. I pushed the button and I spent a horrible time with the lurid stuff that comes through that machine."

He choked up momentarily.

"I felt like dirt. The next morning I got up and I could hardly read my Bible. I just felt like dirt. It was horrible. I just died inside. I couldn't call my wife. I didn't know what to do. Then the next night I did the very same thing on the very same TV set in the very same motel room. I need your help. Would you be willing to really hold me accountable?"

We need to be open to others. Everywhere we look people are dying inside and struggling with difficult problems because they don't have someone to confide in and help them withstand the challenge. While we may be rich materially, modern America is like the church at Laodicea in Revelation 3:14-22—wretched, miserable, poor, blind and naked. Though steeped in money and creature comforts, we are lacking in the relationships that will enrich our lives and society.

> "But we proved to be gentle among you, as a nursing mother tenderly cares for her own children. Having so fond an affection for you, we were well-pleased to impart to you not only the gospel of God but also our own lives, because you had become very dear to us."
> —1 Thessalonians 2:7-8

As Paul pointed out to the Thessalonians, discipleship involves caring, like a nursing mother tenderly feeding her child. When friends stumble, you can shake a finger in their face and lecture them, telling them God makes a way of escape. Or you can offer to hold them up in prayer and reassure them we all fall short in some way.

If you are imparting your life to others, yet hide the struggles with anger, anxiety or other problems you've endured, then you're failing to teach them properly. I've met a number of people who profess to have very few problems. Such folks often have a problem they can't see— pride and arrogance.

Over the years, I have learned to share my problems in life in a discipling relationship. Because there must be a friendship for such a relationship to work, I'm less afraid of revealing the real me during these sessions. In addition, I've seen character being built in my life and in the lives of those I'm working with, be it businessmen, other couples or our children.

Modeling Righteousness

Ever hear someone complaining about children's lack of manners, lack of respect, careless attitudes and unwillingness to work? While it's easy to complain about something we don't like, when it comes to young people we must ask: *Who's to blame?* Is it their fault for not knowing how to act, or their parents' fault for not teaching them?

Discipling our children means presenting a role model for them to follow. Don't expect to cheat on your income tax, knock back six-packs, complain about everything under the sun, be lazy and then expect your children to act better. Diligent parents set an example and look for ways to be involved in their children's lives to help build their character. As they slip and fall, we must offer them ways to get up and avoid falling again.

One thing I have repeatedly emphasized with our children is the need to memorize Scripture. When we get God's Word into our hearts, we can see how God, through the Holy Spirit, will give us the grace to do what He wants us to do. I also stress this with the men I disciple. Memory work helps all of us renew our minds—including the younger generation. Scripture can help them overcome monumental challenges.

You may look at a business owner who is better off financially and say, "Well, he doesn't have the problems that I have." Don't kid yourself. I have seen enough business people up close to know how real and fallible they are, regardless of how much they own or the responsibilities resting on their shoulders. When was it that you think their human susceptibility to temptation and weakness vanished?

A biblical passage that is particularly helpful with overcoming fear, anger and anxiety appears in the second chapter of Philippians. Verses 1-2 advise,

> Therefore if there is any encouragement in Christ, if there is any consolation of love, if there is any fellowship of the Spirit, if any affection and compassion, make my joy complete by being of the same mind, maintaining the same love, united in spirit, intent on one purpose.

It goes on to encourage us to do nothing with selfish or conceited motives, to embrace humility, to regard others as more important than ourselves and to look out for their interests. It discusses encouraging them in Christ, having fellowship of the spirit, unity in outlook and purpose, and maintaining the bonds of love.

In all, these verses list fourteen things to do without grumbling or complaining. I call it a short course in human relations, one which would go miles toward resolving the tension in the nation's homes that has led to the plague of divorce. This is why renewing the mind is so vital to our nation's future.

The other key to raising happy, obedient children is relationship. If you try to instruct solely by rules without building a relationship, you harvest rebellion. When there is a conflict around our house, it is a ready-made signal that I need to carve out some time for my children. They may have a problem I can help solve, or they may be angry because I haven't spent enough time with them.

When I started taking our kids out on dates, they quickly got used to it. There is no substitute for that one-on-one time. The power of one-on-one is absolutely incredible. Young people need to be able to share their struggles with a caring, mature parent. If all Mom or Dad ever come across with are a bunch of dictates and rules, children will either rebel or shut down, clamming up tighter than a bank vault and leaving their parents mystified.

But children respond when their father says, "I really love you. You're just a great kid. I mean, you're just great. I'd have given anything if I could have had a little brother like you. I just think you're the greatest guy in the world." I used to tell our kids, "If I lost your mother, my job, everything I own, and my health, and I just had you, I'd be still be the most blessed man on earth."

That worked until our youngest daughter, Susanna, started growing up and getting wise. One time I repeated the familiar refrain and threw in, "Even if I lose all my clothes and all I have is you, I'll be the most blessed man on earth." Looking at me with a deadpan expression, she said, "They'll arrest you if you don't have any clothes on."

Why are those youngest kids so smart?

Twelve Steps to Modeling Righteousness for Your Children

1. Discipline biblically, in love.
2. Combine father power with mother mercy.
3. Review wrongs, not to criticize but to help the offender achieve power over sin through the indwelling presence of the Holy Spirit.
4. Memorize Scripture verses with them.

5. Teach them the lesson of Philippians 2, to do all things without complaining or grumbling.

6. Be transparent.

7. Don't just review Bible verses. Discuss the principles and desired conduct found in them.

8. Apply Scripture by giving examples of people who have paid consequences for ignoring lessons from the Bible.

9. Don't "protect" children from knowing the results of sin.

10. Teach children how to pray through a Bible verse.

11. Encourage them with plenty of hugs and words of positive encouragement.

12. Give them an opportunity to pass on the principles they are learning to their friends.

Questions for Reflection

1. How would you describe your lifestyle? What would be the benefits of simplifying it or lowering your material standards?

2. Describe your relationship with your father. How is that affecting your actions today?

3. What material possessions did you long for when you were younger? Did you ever get them? How did that make you feel?

4. Outside of your marriage, how many close friendships do you have? How does that make you feel?

5. What temptations do you struggle with? Who holds you accountable to help you overcome them?

6. Which of the "Twelve Steps to Modeling Righteousness" are you teaching your children? What results have you seen?

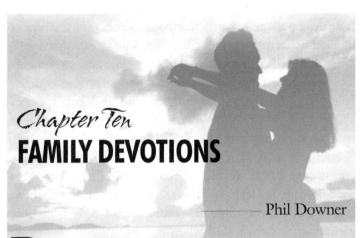

Chapter Ten
FAMILY DEVOTIONS

——————— Phil Downer

R enowned radio teacher and pastor Chuck Swindoll
once told me a story about a group of pastors who
were discussing what had led them into the ministry. They
went around the room, talking about how they were encouraged to walk with God and the path that led them into the
pulpit. But not one person mentioned family devotions.

When a participant recognized that, he stopped and said,
"Wait a minute. Why didn't we talk about family devotions?"
That sparked additional discussion. The group's consensus:
They were boring. Force-fed a steady diet of family devotions, they didn't like them. If that's how a group of church
leaders felt about their experience as youngsters, imagine the
challenge you face! You may have children (or a spouse) who
moan about having to attend services regularly, be it on
Sunday or one of the alternatives springing up today.

Nothing will challenge your creativity and resourcefulness
more than leading these devotional sessions. Imagine sitting
down with an unruly crew. One is almost asleep on the table
while a second chomps on a snack, another is kicking her feet
and a fourth bangs the table while grinning, "Hi, Dad!" Then

your mate walks in, groans, "You mean we're doing this now? I thought we were doing this at 8 o'clock. Can't we do this later?"

Under such circumstances, the old male ego can quickly kick into gear. If you're not careful, you may find yourself bellowing, "Let's quit fooling around and get it done! We're going to teach the Word! Pay attention now while I try to cram something into your heads!"

Such an explosion may crack the whip on obstinate youngsters, but it won't guarantee they'll listen (probably the opposite, in fact). And it certainly won't endear them to learning about the Bible. Speaking as a man, I know how easily men get frustrated when it seems nobody is paying attention or respecting your authority. Leading dynamic family devotions demands creativity and resourcefulness, topped off by huge mounds of patience.

While much of this chapter will deal with involving your children in Bible study and discussion, don't forget this habit also helps develop your marriage. One of the best ways to build intimacy in a marriage is through spiritual connections. This is a two-way street. Husbands don't own all the best insights. God has blessed women with intuition and better relationship sense. They can see things in biblical parables and episodes that men might miss.

There should be a leader. Whether that is the husband or the wife, or you want to alternate these duties, someone has to be "in charge." But think of yourself as a facilitator, not an iron-fisted know-it-all. Don't overlook your spouse in the process. As you complement and reinforce each other's insights, you will be teaching your children two lessons:

- That you respect each other and so should they.
- That the Bible is the most important guidebook for their lives.

Make It Fun

One of the best ways for parents to model good behavior and teach how to make right choices is through family devotions. For our family it is a time of fantastic togetherness. We look at the Scriptures and we pray together. It is a time of encouragement and—believe it or not—fun. I've done some crazy things over the years to teach different points from the Bible.

To use a popular modern phrase, think interactively. Get your children involved in discussions and applying concepts they read about. With young children, aim for about ten percent content and ninety percent discussion.

> The first rule of good family devotions is: *Thou shalt not bore everyone to death.* Don't sit there and blandly instruct, "OK, we're going to turn to Ezekiel now and read the first fifteen chapters." This is a time for encouragement and fun. The Bible has the best stories ever written. Don't make them dry as dust.

Try one verse, or even one word, like *humility, kindness* or *love*. Draw your children out. Encourage them to think about what they mean in practical terms. How can they put such concepts into practice?

Once you lay the groundwork in their early years, it will be amazing how that seed grows. With our older children, we can go really deep. Abigail, Paul and Matthew have done detailed studies of books like Romans. It's a "line

upon line, precept upon precept" (see Isaiah 28:10, NIV)
approach come to life.

Children are eager to learn. It's up to parents to make the
context interesting. Susy and I like to bring the Bible to life by
sharing stories, whether from the newspaper, people around
us or episodes from our lives. We sometimes change the
names to protect others' privacy, but use plenty of stories.

> "The Lord's bond-servant must not be
> quarrelsome, but be kind to all,
> able to teach, patient when wronged,
> with gentleness correcting those who
> are in opposition, if perhaps God
> may grant them repentance leading
> to the knowledge of the truth."
> —2 Timothy 2:24-25

Family devotions is such a precious time that whoever
ignores it is missing out on a pearl of great value. As parents, it is our job to relate lessons from God's perspective to
our children. Our worldly culture won't do it.

We have used devotion times to warn them about the
consequences of sin and the results of wrong-doing that
can tear their lives apart. We describe the pictures they will
never see on television.

Sometimes I take the lesson past the dining room table.
Although our children were very young at the time, I once
drove them to a junkyard. Our oldest daughter still vividly
remembers seeing a red sports car, crunched like a pancake,
beer cans still lying on the floor. The smashed windshield

and the blood covering the dashboard made an impression that outlived a thousand lectures.

I try not to fill these sessions with nothing but frowning, doom-and-gloom warnings. Shaking a finger all the time may create an appetite in curious young minds to sample the sin as soon as they're old enough. But I have patiently explained how millions of homes have been divided by people choosing their own way over God's way.

> Spiritual progress with your children will come in bite-sized pieces. But don't give up. Down the road, you will be happy you stuck with it.

We sometimes discuss relationships. We have talked about close friends going through a divorce and how painful it was to everyone concerned. We described how they had the same kind of relationship struggles as our family but didn't resolve them. Some parents think they should shield their children from unpleasantness, but I don't agree. God loves each of us, but he hates our sin and doesn't relieve us of the consequences of our actions.

At the heart of each discussion is Scripture. We can all give our opinion or talk about what others think, but what really matters is what God says. Help your children examine issues from God's perspective. Describe the consequences of following God—the fruit and joy of that decision—and the consequences of going man's way.

Don't get intimidated. I must confess that I have made a lot of mistakes during devotions. When confronted with scenes like I mentioned earlier, it took a long time to get over the habit of slapping the table and shouting, "Stop that!"

On other occasions I've come out in a hurry to get to work and tried to rush through a lesson. Suddenly Susy would interrupt with something like, "No, I think it was the Israelites, not the Armenians." That usually intimidates or embarrasses me or induces self-pity, touching off an argument in front of the kids. More than once I've had to go into the bedroom and pray, then come back and apologize.

Don't overlook the value of questions. One day we were discussing the biblical principle of obedience. I described how a man at work had been giving me a lot of problems because he wouldn't follow my directives. Then I asked, "What do you think about that? What do you think I ought to do about this situation?"

"You ought to fire him," piped up one child.

"Well," I said, "how would it feel if you didn't do your job around here and I fired you?"

"Oh, yeah, not so good," he replied. "Well, maybe you ought to talk to him."

"Maybe you ought to pray about it before you talk to him," said another. "Maybe you ought to ask him some questions and find out what's going on in his life. Maybe you ought to consider whether you're doing your job right. Maybe you could enable him to do his job better."

Not only have our children learned about scriptural principles through daily devotions, they have received informal lessons in personnel management. They have learned to think through situations before reacting. They know how to apply biblical reasoning to their daily lives. Progress comes in bite-sized pieces, so is often difficult to see, but the rewards will be there.

Start with Quiet Time

Families used to be the center of fun. In days gone by, fathers came home from work and everyone gathered around the dining room table for dinner and the day's news. Everyone got tidbits of information from the rest of the family. Sadly, in the twenty-first century, electronic media have supplanted the family. Most of our news comes from cable and news networks, radio or the Internet.

So much of what used to bring families together has been discarded. It takes intentional effort to remain a cohesive unit. Family devotions can be a time of sharing joy about the Lord and what He's doing in our lives. If we want our kids to grow up knowing Scripture, the most important thing we can do is model devotion to God's Word.

> Modern culture surrounds us and profoundly influences our lives. But it doesn't mean you are helpless. You can swim against the tides. With planning and determination, you can raise your children to appreciate God's Word.

Remember, this habit isn't just for the children. One day they will be grown and on their own. That will not be the time for you and your spouse to kick up your heels and forget the Bible. You should plan on growing together spiritually for the rest of your lives. The headlines have been full of those who failed to do so and saw their marriages crumble after twenty, thirty or forty years.

A question you may be asking is, *How? How can I find the time? My day is already crammed full of activities. How can I squeeze anything else into it?* Well, can you find the time if it means that you enjoy a lifelong marriage, until death do you part? Is it worth taking the time if your children grow into strong servants of the Lord and raise your grandchildren to do the same?

If you want to know the secret of success, check out the first chapter of Joshua. This book is about one of the greatest leaders in biblical history. Joshua was a man who spoke his mind and led the nation of Israel into the Promised Land. Whoever your military or political hero may be, few can compare with this leader.

> When I first became a Christian, I thought I was "spiritual." In reality, I was spiritually immature. Only by reading God's Word and praying did I learn how to follow Him and discern His will for my life.

In verse 6, the Lord tells Joshua, "Be strong and courageous, because you will lead these people to inherit the land I swore to their forefathers to give them" (NIV). He goes on in verse 7 to warn, "Be strong and very courageous. Be careful to obey all the law my servant Moses gave you; do not turn from it to the right or to the left, that you may be successful wherever you go" (NIV). God tells Joshua to meditate on His law continually and follow its ways, because "then you will be prosperous and successful" (1:8, NIV).

Do you want your children to be successful? Here is the formula: God admonishes us to follow His Word and then we will know what to do. The Bible must be a crucial element of our daily lives and central to our existence. I saw this truth after some of my early, fumbling attempts to be a "good Christian."

When I first accepted Christ as my Savior and Lord, I thought that made me spiritual. In truth, I was spiritually immature. My life exhibited some old principles and a lot of ruts and misguided thinking. However, it is difficult to change yourself. The key was Jim, the man I've previously mentioned, whom God sent to disciple me—a spiritual father in the person of a doctor who disliked lawyers but loved me.

This doctor, with a wife, four children and a busy medical practice that required him to be on call every other night and alternate weekends, made time to meet with me once a week. Because I became "very dear" to him, Jim walked with me, cried with me and showed me how to study the Bible, pray and seek God.

Thanks to his instruction, I realized how much I had to learn. I saw that I didn't know how to get rid of my bad habits or how to know God's will for my life. I knew I wanted more of God, so Jim encouraged me to spend more time in His Word. As I did that, He changed me. As Paul wrote, "Do not conform any longer to the pattern of this world, but be transformed by the renewing of your mind" (Romans 12:2, NIV). I set out to accomplish this goal.

I started with a morning quiet time. At first I wasn't too faithful. I might say a quick prayer, listen to a Christian radio station on the way to work and exclaim in the parking lot, "Jesus, just help me today." I got out of it what I put into it—and sometimes I didn't get much. My time with God particularly faltered when I was facing courtroom pressure. Things didn't go too well outside the courtroom, either.

From this shallow spiritual experience, I learned I could let God carry my load and work with Him, or try to carry it myself and stagger under the weight. I saw how much I needed a daily quiet time to talk with the Lord and listen for His still, small voice or detect His speaking through the Bible. This time matures us as Christians. We can't hope to lead dynamic family devotions—or our lives—without it.

> If you're having trouble finding time to read the Bible in the morning, start by measuring one inch of Scripture. Read it, ask God to show you a truth from it and say a quick prayer. That's better than nothing.

I may fast occasionally from physical food, but I never abstain from spiritual food. I literally feast on the Word. Over the years, I have increased the time, doubling and re-doubling it. It means getting up early, but anything worth having takes sacrifice.

If you are struggling to establish this habit, I recommend following the "one inch rule." When I battled a busy court schedule, I got started by opening the New Testament and reading the equivalent of one inch of Scripture. Then I prayed for a minute. It was amazing how God used that in my life. Before long I was thirsting to read more and my appetite steadily grew. As God revealed more truth, it inspired me to get up even earlier—and I had never been a "morning" person.

True Confessions

Susy and I have seen many benefits in our lives from having a quiet time. I can't overemphasize its importance. It is the cornerstone of all that goes on the rest of the day. In addition to growing spiritually through quiet times with the Lord, I have also grown through striving to make His character part of mine. Often He directed me to do things I wouldn't have otherwise.

For example, one of the hardest things I have ever done is humble myself before our children. You can't imagine how tough it is to call them together and admit, "I really blew it. I lost track of my focus. I was starting to get too carried away with things at work. I focused on the task instead of you. Would you please forgive me? It must really hurt you when I lose my temper."

It is truly amazing what kind of bonds such a confession builds. As you humble yourself, you are modeling the kind of conduct you want from your children. Once you lay this kind of groundwork, you stand a much better chance of establishing fun family devotions. If this sounds too difficult, start by sweating a few drops of blood (just kidding). And remember, this didn't come easy for me, either.

Leading family devotions in the morning meant I couldn't get to the office early. But I had to determine that I would have a significant impact in our children's lives—and maybe not be so successful at work. Surprise! That didn't happen. When I started spending time in the Word with our children, I didn't need as much time to get things done at the office. God multiplied my effectiveness.

I hope this episode of "True Confessions" doesn't discourage you. More often than I care to admit, I have failed terribly. I have gotten upset over minor irritations or Susy's correcting me when I didn't think it was necessary. And sometimes I just blew my stack and lost my cool.

Once I got mad in the middle of a devotional session. Repeated instances of childish behavior and "no respect" sent me up the wall. Losing my temper, I stormed out of the room and out the front door. Slamming the door, I climbed into my car and tossed my briefcase on the backseat before driving away. All the kids were stunned. Finally, one shrugged, "Well, there goes Dad. Great devotions, huh?"

> ## Once I got so mad during our devotionals I stormed out of the house and drove away. The kids sat there stunned. Finally someone said, "Well, there goes Dad. Great devotions, huh?"

Driving down the street, I threw one of the best pity parties I had ever attended. Huffing and puffing, I snarled, "Boy, I just don't deserve this. I'm killing myself to put this stuff together and nobody appreciates it. Not the kids and not Susy. Nobody cares. I just don't deserve this."

In the twinkling of an eye, it seemed as if the Lord had picked up a megaphone, even though the only sound was a quiet thought crawling through my brain. "Phil, remember that I hung on the cross for you, big guy. You pierced my hands and feet. What do you mean, you don't deserve this? I gave you these kids to train."

Even that commanding voice didn't bring my misery to a halt. It took some more "poor me's" and "I can't do this" before I came to my senses. I had to decide whether to be a slave of righteousness or a defeated slave to my flesh. If I wanted to serve Christ, I had to turn the car around and go home. When I got to the driveway, I muttered, "I hate this. I just hate having to say, 'I'm sorry.' "

Swallowing hard, I walked in and said, "Guys, I'm sorry. I really blew it. Would somebody pray for me?" Then we finished our discussion. Men, the Lord says we are to be the spiritual leaders of our homes. And we will lead—either upward or downward. We're either good or bad. When we exercise self-control over our feelings, our children learn to do the same. If we vent lots of steam, they learn that too.

Family devotions have not come easily. But I had to vow to do them at all costs. If necessary, write out your pledge and put the note where you can see it constantly. Do we have devotions every day? Every day I'm home, if at all possible. Every home experiences some kind of emergency or unavoidable interruption. The goal is consistency, not putting a check mark on a calendar every day.

Over the years it has become much easier. I've learned a lot. For parents who are concerned with teaching their children eternal values, my advice is to avoid taking yourself too seriously. Find a scriptural truth, but mix it with ninety percent jokes, fun and encouragement. The Bible is full of appealing messages and inspiration. What more could you want? As I mentioned, the goal as parents is to be a team in teaching your children. Susy will finish this chapter by sharing more about what has worked for us.

Making Devotions Work

———— Susy Downer

There are many devotional books available that are very helpful. Say you need some ideas on age-appropriate issues to discuss with your children. There are so many that it would take too much space to list them all. Consult a local Christian bookstore for suggestions. That is one way to start, especially if you lack confidence. Better to use a book or study guide than to avoid the task completely.

> "If you, then, though you are evil, know how to give good gifts to your children, how much more will your Father in heaven give good gifts to those who ask him!"
> —Matthew 7:11, NIV

Still, I believe in the simple power of the Word. One of our most interesting and productive exercises is to select a favorite Proverb or Psalm. We go around in a circle and have everyone read a verse or two, then explain it in their own words. Even small children with an easily read version of the Bible can do that.

Encourage your children to talk about the meaning of the chapter or verse and ask some questions. A good study

Bible may give you ideas for additional questions or may help stimulate your discussion. In the beginning, it isn't important that children have profound thoughts or gain vast amounts of knowledge. The idea is to make them feel a part of the community of the family and to whet their appetite for more. You are setting a pattern for the future.

Aside from our family devotions, we encourage our children to develop their own quiet time. I have been thrilled with the insights they have gained during their private sessions with God. Occasionally Phil has said, "Well, why don't we all share what we got out of our quiet time this morning?" At first a few had blank looks on their faces, but they quickly learned they didn't want to repeat the experience.

> Our devotional times have been a key factor in teaching our children to think and reason, and not just about the Bible, but about life in general. They have also learned discipline during these sessions.

These little surprises have been a great reminder not to let their minds wander. All of us are tempted to drift through our quiet time so we can get on with the rest of our day. Asking them about what they learned helps develop a focus on Scripture. And it helps keep us on our toes too, because they won't let us get away without describing our own insights.

While this is a good habit to develop for the rest of their lives, we don't do this to "test" them. Our discussions are vital times of encouragement. These aren't sessions to criticize our children's opinions or interpretations of Scripture. I think our devotional times have been a key factor in teaching our children to think and reason, and not just about the Bible, but about life in general.

For Christmas recently we gave each of them YWAM's (Youth With A Mission) *Personal Prayer Diary Daily Planner*. Having each of their names engraved on the front made it even more special. They were thrilled. Only Paul had established journaling as a daily discipline over the past six years and I wanted to encourage the others to either begin or to be more consistent. This planner has a place for recording prayers and daily Bible insights. It also has several plans for reading the Bible in one year, articles on quiet time and spiritual warfare, and encouragement to pray for people groups across the world. Praying as a family will give your children a focus beyond themselves.

Another thing that helps them develop biblical insights is Phil's asking follow-up questions. He also won't let them make broad generalizations that can't be supported by Scripture or other facts. He isn't trying to criticize or find fault, but to help them reason through their statements.

Our children have learned discipline during devotions too. You have probably caught an inkling of my husband's strict nature. I still have vivid memories of sitting around the table when most of the children were still pretty young. They would be fidgeting, wiggling and making sounds. He would smack the table with his palm, startling them.

"Look at me, children," he would say. And they did! His smile let them know he wasn't angry, but he was serious about wanting them to focus. Once he had their attention, it amazed me how still they sat and how long they watched and listened. Even at tender ages they could sit and listen for extended periods of time. Granted, youngsters generally have short attention spans, but that is too often a convenient excuse for never training them to sit quietly or pay attention. As a result they never develop self-discipline.

However, you and your mate need to discuss—and agree on—methods of keeping order ahead of time. I can say this because of the battles we endured over this issue. With my motherly, protective instincts in full bloom, I sometimes moaned, "Honey, I think you're being too hard on them. They're just too little to understand. They're bored. They don't know what you're talking about. Especially the younger ones."

> Our two youngest children (at the time) sat in family devotions for more than four years and rarely said a word. But once they started discussing things and expressing their opinions, I saw how much they had absorbed before they spoke.

Some days I was pretty disparaging of his efforts. I regret that, because now I can see how his leadership worked. As the one who does most of the homeschooling, I am reaping the benefits of that early discipline. In my misguided compassion, I would have gone a lot easier on the children and they wouldn't have developed good, orderly habits, not to mention the ability to reason and discuss the important issues of Scripture.

From the time they were three until they reached seven, our twins sat in devotions and rarely said a word. They only spoke if Phil asked them a question. I honestly thought they weren't getting anything out of it. Suddenly, between the ages of seven and eight, they started commenting and asking questions. It was like watching flowers bloom.

Their eager participation showed how wrong I was; they had been absorbing much more than I believed. Once they were mature and articulate enough, they had the confidence to interact with their older brothers and sisters. This made me grateful they hadn't missed devotions during those formative years when I would have just let them go out and play.

Sharing Your Self

Phil mentioned earlier that he shares stories about the office during family devotions. These sessions are a time for sharing ourselves, which we have carried into other areas of our parenting. For example, he suggested a goal, which I adopted as well, that we teach our children most of the practical things we know before they leave home.

This means such things as household tasks, personnel issues and dealing with finances. Phil tells them about various decisions and struggles he has faced in the office. He began years ago, while he was still practicing law.

I believe fathers should spend more time sharing about their occupation with their children. Little ones need to understand some of the demands and problems their parents deal with so they are prepared for the world of work. In our Bible clubs I have asked many children, "What does your father do?" and they have no idea. They don't know where he works, what he does or what kinds of challenges he faces.

I don't emphasize this point because I believe in daily vocational training. Too many children grow up strangers to a person they ought to know intimately. Even if the day-to-day details would bore them, children can still learn about issues surrounding your work. You can explain inter-personal relationships, your company's product or service and its contribution to society.

Fathers, if you ask the Lord to show you, God will reveal lessons from your work that you can teach your children. It may be some practical information or a spiritual lesson. You will be amazed at how much you can teach them—not to mention how much more interested they will be in what you are doing.

When Phil has grappled with sticky details or situations at work, he tells us so we can all pray about it. If your company is struggling, let your children share that burden. You don't have to spell out every detail, especially if it might frighten them. But if you're stressed out and acting strange, they're going to sense something is wrong anyway.

> ## "And all the people would get up early in the morning to come to [Christ] in the temple to listen to Him."
> ### —Luke 21:38

Over the years, we expanded our devotions to about an hour. We don't always spend the whole session on Bible study. We may weave in stories or discuss something of concern coming up that day. If Phil needs prayer support about a meeting, he mentions it. Any challenge someone in the family has that day is a topic for prayer. After discussion, we go around the room and each person prays. It has been a wonderful way to start our day.

A caution: If you're going to get up early to do devotions and let your husband get to work on time, plan ahead. You have to get to bed the night before if you expect to have devotions without being tired and crabby. We moms often don't have a minute to ourselves until the kids go to bed. Then we can think of fifty things we need to do. It is extremely tempting to stay up late and get them done. But then we may be too tired in the morning.

You can't imagine how many times Phil and I wrestled over my early-morning sleepiness. One day he said, "Susy, you know how grateful you say you are for me doing this? You're the biggest impediment I have to doing devotions."

That really hurt my feelings. If I had wanted to throw a good, old-fashioned temper tantrum, I had adequate ammunition. But as I thought it over, I had to admit it was true. I hadn't been very supportive. I had to acknowledge my failure to myself, to him and to God, then make an effort to change.

I still blow it sometimes, especially if we have out-of-town guests and get out of sync. But it's when we have relatives or old friends over, who may not be used to this routine, that we need these times the most. Every time we get off schedule, I get some practical insight about why having family devotions is such a worthwhile habit. After all these years, I still need reminders of what is most important.

I encourage you to start small and work your way up. Trust the Lord, make it fun and don't be afraid to ask your children what they want to do. As Phil has said, the most important thing is to do it and to do it with joy. Give your children and your marriage a vital boost for the future.

Questions for Reflection

1. Did your family have devotions when you were a child? How has that affected your outlook on Bible study?

2. If you didn't have devotions growing up, was there someone else who taught you about Scripture? How do you feel about that person today?

3. What forces are pulling your family apart? What steps can you take to have more meaningful times together?

4. Do you consider getting up early to do Bible study a legalistic requirement? If so, when do you make time for family devotions?

5. Did your parents ever apologize for losing their tempers or making mistakes? How did that make you feel?

6. Do your children look up to you? If so, what kind of impression do you think sharing your biblical insights will make on them?

7. If you don't do family devotions, what is the biggest obstacle to starting them? How can you overcome this obstacle?

Chapter Eleven
LIFESTYLE EVANGELISM

———— Phil Downer

E ver try to make friends with your next-door neighbor or a couple down the street so you could tell them about Christ? When some friends in another city did, they were shocked at what they discovered. "Larry" and "Sharon" had just watched an excellent video entitled *Living Proof— Lifestyle Evangelism*, which is a series of lessons on sharing your faith. A follow-up series, entitled *Lifestyle Discipleship*, looks at the challenges of discipleship and how to disciple friends, relatives, business colleagues and neighbors.

After finishing the lessons, Larry and Sharon decided to put them into practice and reach out to the couple next door. It didn't take long to discover this couple's marriage was a royal mess. Climbing beyond the emotional walls the couple had erected proved a formidable task. Trying as gently as possible, all the while showing love and concern, Larry and Sharon just couldn't penetrate those barriers. Nevertheless, they kept on loving their neighbors.

One day, the wife came over to Larry and Sharon's home, bawling. Her husband had just told her that he was involved with another woman. Sprawled across the kitchen table, weeping, she ranted and raved and made suicidal threats. The scene seemed almost surreal—the scenarios Sharon had watched on video were coming to life in front of her eyes. Fortunately she was ready to share the answer of Jesus Christ with this wounded wife.

Sharon didn't just give simple, pat answers. She listened as the woman poured her heart out, then offered her sympathy and told this wife the secret of what had rescued her own life. Sharon succeeded in leading her to Christ, but that wasn't the end of the story. In communities of the twenty-first century, there's usually more. If anything, it gets worse. A lot of twisted, crazy, unbelievable things are taking place in modern-day America.

The affair continued and the other woman became pregnant by the woman's husband. That threw a whole new twist into Sharon's discipling efforts. Here was a brand-new Christian trying to patch her life back together and find reassurance that God would meet her needs, and she gets sucker-punched by reality. To make matters worse, months later the woman who had the affair with her husband brought the baby by the house to parade her love child in front of the wife and her children. It made those old soap operas like *Peyton Place* and *Melrose Place* look tame.

The husband was ready to check out and leave his family, the other woman and the whole town behind. He couldn't imagine dealing with worse humiliation. But Larry took a risk and built a relationship with this man. He didn't act shocked, smirk or display a condescending attitude when the man confessed the sordid truth of his mistakes over breakfast.

Larry told him how, without the Lord's correction, he might have wandered down a similar path. He encouraged the husband and promised that the situation could improve. Months later, he led the man to receive Jesus as his Savior.

Was that the end of this troubled couple's problems? Hardly. Sin has its consequences and the Lord doesn't relieve us of our consequences. The hurt, pain, emotional carnage and lingering resentment over the affair left a ton of personal problems to be resolved.

Larry and Sharon walked through the pain with them. They patiently discipled the couple, honestly discussed their own past hurts and fears and constantly reassured them that God hadn't written them off because of their mistakes.

> Getting involved in your neighbors' or coworkers' lives may lead you into the midst of some shocking, personally revolting situations. But our mission is to rescue people from the sordid results of living apart from God.

What happened next is nothing short of a miracle. I don't offer this as some kind of standard or suggest that anyone else try it. I'm just relating what happened because it is such a powerful testimony of how Jesus Christ changes people from the inside out.

The young wife found it in her heart to forgive her husband, the other woman and to accept their child. She recognized that if God forgave her, she couldn't live with resentment for a helpless infant. Then she took it a step further, saying she felt the Lord leading her to pray about adopting the baby. Since then, she has filed formal adoption papers.

An astonishing story, yet one that could easily have ended in tragedy, violence and even death were it not for a caring couple taking time to comfort their troubled neighbors. Imagine this happy ending compared to the outcome of most families experiencing a personal crisis.

This is the result of lifestyle evangelism—Christians sharing their faith and being willing to get involved in the dirty details, chaos and dysfunctional lives of their neighbors and coworkers. All so they can share the answer to life's problems.

> "And when I came to you, brethren, I did not come with superiority of speech or of wisdom, proclaiming to you the testimony of God. For I determined to know nothing among you except Jesus Christ, and Him crucified."
> —1 Corinthians 2:1-2

Your children need to see you sharing your faith. Hearing you talk about witnessing for Christ at church but never seeing you take the time to tell someone on your block can leave them cynical and disillusioned. You also want to teach them how to go about this with their friends and classmates.

Living at Home

Women who stay at home to raise their children represent a dying breed in our nation. I understand that there are some women who must work, including single mothers and those whose husbands simply don't earn enough to support their family. Everyone goes through some tough times. If you're doing what God has led you to do, then my comments shouldn't upset you.

But there are also many working for the privilege of having more things or because they are striving to live up to society's ideals. Today's American culture broadcasts the message, "You're not doing anything productive because you're not a lawyer" or "because you're not in sales," or "Because you're not a secretary, you're not doing anything. All you're doing is staying at home."

Right. All stay-at-home mothers are doing is nurturing and training their children, raising the nation's next generation of leaders. That happens to be the most important job in the world. I can't find a Scripture that says, "Go unto all the world and be lawyers," or "Go out into all the world and train people how to sell insurance." Jesus told us to go and make disciples.

The highest and best option for discipling is right in our own home and within our own neighborhood. Not to mention what a blessing it is when children are raised by their mothers who are there for them during the day and after school. I don't want to say that is the only option, but neither should we denigrate this honorable, demanding profession like society has for the past three decades.

Susy and a lot of full-time mothers could be driving new cars, getting pats on the back at the office and buying new dresses on payday. Instead, no one sees them as they stand in front of their office: two machines that wash and dry. Oh, the children might, but most of them won't appreciate Mom's effort until they're grown and have to do their own laundry.

Mothers who commit to stay home and raise the future leaders of our churches, ministries, families and government deserve our thanks and hearty applause. One time I did this at a large prayer breakfast in California. They were honoring doctors, lawyers and judges. I thought we should honor the folks who stayed at home to raise these leaders—and said so.

Some people grew pretty upset with me as they described their plight. But I wasn't attacking them. I was simply trying to shine the spotlight on our unsung heroes. Mothers deserve more recognition than one day a year. Those who stay home are bearing a much tougher load than people at the office can imagine.

> "Charm is deceitful and beauty is vain, but a woman who fears the LORD, she shall be praised. Give her the product of her hands, and let her works praise her in the gates."
> —Proverbs 31:30-31

You might wonder what stay-at-home mothers have to do with lifestyle evangelism. Everything. If we had more women at home with their children during the day, we would have more stable neighborhoods and more examples of the benefits of a life centered on Christ instead of on things.

This is why I'm also a firm believer that men should do more to bear the enormous workload at home. Fathers who sit around at home and excuse their inactivity by saying they've worked all day ignore the fact that mothers rarely rest until after the lights go out. Many men need to grow up and shoulder more domestic responsibility.

Until I enlisted in the marine corps, I didn't know how to sew on a button or wash a shirt. I thought the way to clean clothes was by throwing them on the floor. That was the system in our home. I threw them on the floor and the next day they showed up in my dresser drawer—cleaned, folded and pressed. Simple, no sweat.

The marines taught me a lot and I started to learn to do some things on my own too. I think we need to teach our sons how to do some domestic chores so they don't have to take the same kind of crash course. It will give them some useful skills, help them to avoid being helpless bachelors and make them better husbands one day.

> "So husbands ought also to love their own wives as their own bodies. He who loves his own wife loves himself; for no one ever hated his own flesh, but nourishes and cherishes it, just as Christ also does the church."
> —Ephesians 5:28-29

I encourage husbands to find ways to help their wives—for example, do the grocery shopping. It's very inefficient for eight different people in our house to run to the store. Frankly, Susy handles that chore for us. I tried but we spent too much money and wound up with the wrong supplies. However, you may be like my wife's father, who manages his household's shopping.

Not only may you be an efficient shopper, this could become an excellent time for a date with one of your children. Great conversations can take place over the lettuce and tomatoes. Your teenagers may be pretty inventive too. When my kids went with me, it was truly amazing what wound up in our cart. I've used the same old soap, hair spray, razor blades and toothpaste for years. The children added variety to our lives.

What about your wife's car? Could you help her clean it out? That can be quite a job. Mine looks pretty clean because I'm like a drill sergeant. With me, it's, "All right, pick up everything. Nobody gets out of here until you pick up what you brought in. If it isn't part of the car, pick it up and get it out of here."

With Susy's car it's a different story. There is stuff crawling out from under the doors. The kids leave behind ice cream sticks, candy wrappers, tin foil off gum wrappers and an assortment of junk. Plus she has her own tissue boxes, old mail and other odds and ends in there. Cleaning it is a monumental task. But Susy really appreciates it when I do it, and you may find your wife feels the same way.

My biggest domestic accomplishment was attacking the clothes pile. Washing, drying and sorting for eight people is tough. Truthfully, I also got tired of putting two black socks in the laundry and getting back one white and one black. That is disturbing when it's time to pack for a trip. I travel a lot and am highly organized. I want to throw everything in the suitcase and leave. That's hard to do when I have to go searching for things.

Plus I wear sweats to jog every morning. A week's collection of that stuff makes up a few loads alone. So I started doing my own wash. I'm up early to run, so I started taking clothes and piling them into the washer before hitting the streets. I use simplified methods. Women worry too much about separating everything. I figure once it's been washed two or three times, the colors aren't going to run, so I dump everything into the washing machine (and I've never had a problem).

I also got organized. I went to the local discount store and bought a stack of snap-together plastic storage units. I call them my clothes condo. Each shelf and box has its purpose—underwear, shirts, jogging suits and so forth. I dirty it, I wash it. When it's clean it goes back in place and when I'm ready to leave town I'm not frantically searching for my stuff. And it drastically cut down on Susy's laundry duties.

Exporting What Is Valuable ——— Susy Downer

When Phil left the legal world for full-time ministry, I didn't think we needed to study yet another course on evangelism. I had already been through plenty of them. But I found the Living Proof series, which Phil mentioned at the beginning of this chapter, to be the most effective lifestyle evangelism tool I have ever studied.

The first video in the Living Proof series, *Lifestyle Evangelism,* includes a workbook and Bible study that are excellent for home groups. The video portion only takes fifteen minutes, and it effectively illustrates one or more of the questions posed during the lesson. These are very down-to-earth portrayals. We found ourselves laughing and crying at the mistakes the Christians made and the trauma the people they're witnessing to endured. You see yourself in it and live it with them.

Earlier Phil mentioned the follow-up video, *Lifestyle Discipleship*. The setting is about ten years later. It shows half a dozen generations of Christians, their disciples and how their lives have intermingled. It is an exciting story. The first time Phil and I watched the videos, we turned them on, popped some popcorn and watched them like a three-hour movie. They are that powerful. You won't find anything better at your local video store.

> "The Lord GOD has given Me the tongue of disciples, that I may know how to sustain the weary one with a word. He awakens Me morning by morning, He awakens My ear to listen as a disciple."
> —Isaiah 50:4

These kinds of studies provide the framework for training and discussions that just won't take place during casual conversations. We have discovered that some people have a desire to do evangelism but have certain unresolved struggles in their own lives. These personal problems won't allow them the freedom to step out and share with their neighbors.

One thing that is so outstanding about these videos is they provide models for people to follow. That is vital if you haven't had the benefit of being discipled yourself. It also allows you and your small group to work through some issues that might otherwise never be addressed.

For example, one session in *Lifestyle Discipleship* deals with the question, "What if you never received your father's blessing?" Another lesson looks at a person struggling with pornography; there is one about a woman dealing with her religion's legalism. The video also examines other issues like materialism and the trauma of losing your job.

If people are willing to be transparent with their friends, family or church group, they can discuss some heartfelt issues and let the Lord heal some of those hurts. A lot of people have completed this training as part of their Sunday school class. One caution: We have found that it isn't quite as effective in Sunday school because people tend not to be as faithful in attendance. They may make a couple of sessions and then miss a couple of classes.

On the positive side, in Sunday schools a couple will often catch a vision for the series. They will take it home and start leading a small group. Five or six couples is an ideal size for this kind of study. A group that size is large enough to stimulate discussion and small enough to promote close interaction.

We strongly believe in the importance of sharing with neighbors. If the people living closest to you don't get to know you, they can't see what kind of difference the Lord makes. If this hasn't been a part of your life yet, Phil and I encourage you to take some kind of lifestyle evangelism training and put it to use. Training is an essential part of becoming a good witness.

You might be surprised at how children can pick up these concepts at a very young age. When we did Living Proof for the first time, Abigail, Paul and Matthew were eleven, nine and seven, respectively. We met each week with a family who had three children of similar ages, plus three teenagers. These young people caught the vision of sharing their faith with their friends. Abigail has since told us that she used to feel guilty because she wasn't sharing her faith like she knew she should. She worried about offending someone, turning him off or ruining their relationship. But Living Proof changed her thinking by giving her the confidence to do what God calls each Christian to do.

One lesson that made an impact on Abigail talked about our being "insiders"—we have the inside track when it comes to influencing certain people. Our daughter saw how the same was true in her own life. With some friends and acquaintances, she had a better opening to reach them than pastors, teachers or other adults. Once she appreciated the influence she had with her friends, it encouraged her to carry out the Great Commission.

Upon completion of the series, our children said, "So how are we going to reach out to our friends?" Since we homeschool, most of their nonchurch friends came from their baseball and softball teams, and energetic practices and games didn't leave much time for the kids to share their faith. I asked them if they wanted to start a Good News Club like we had had in Atlanta before moving to Tennessee. They were enthusiastic.

Child Evangelism Fellowship (CEF) sponsors Good News Clubs in 151 countries around the world. They publish incredibly effective material to teach the Word of God and present the gospel in an interesting, compelling manner. The Bible studies come with flannelgraphs which our children cut out and presented with the story. CEF also publishes exciting missionary stories and songs in large notebook form that can be held up in front of the children during meetings.

The children invited their friends (Good News Clubs are most effective for ages six to eleven) and I followed up with the parents. Each of our five older children assumed different responsibilities during our meetings. Then twelve, Abigail taught the missionary story. Paul (ten) and Anna (six) did the flannelgraphs while Matthew (eight) and Joshua (six) helped lead the singing. I took the lead on the Bible story, but asked each of the children to memorize a portion. I nodded to them when it was their turn to stand and share.

Initially they were stiff as boards and had to read their sentences off a card. But over the months and years they improved immensely. They learned to be comfortable sharing their faith with their friends, including those who were skeptical. During the three years we did the club in Chattanooga, we had about fifteen children yield their lives to Christ. There is nothing as exciting as seeing a new child of Christ; this made an indelible impression on our children. They are forever "hooked" on the privilege and reward of being a part of someone accepting the Lord.

I encourage you to help your children form a Good News Club and accomplish many things simultaneously. You are discipling your children in the tenets of their faith, training them to share that faith with others, teaching them that ministry has many aspects (such as cleaning up, fixing refreshments and sharing toys) and that the home makes a wonderful environment for evangelism and discipleship. You also prepare them to feel comfortable speaking in front of a group of people. Our formerly tongue-tied little children now speak confidently at conferences with audiences of several hundred people. Many think they have a gift for speaking, but actually it was pure training, starting with stumbling through a few sentences in front of their friends.

Being a Good Neighbor

You may have a desire to get to know other families in your neighborhood but just don't know how to reach out to them. In the cyberspeed-paced world in which we live, people are constantly busy. The margin in our lives is so small that people have, as a general rule, little time to take on new activities, regardless of their value. People are just doing what they have to do to survive.

What we have discovered is that when the Lord has laid a family or individual on our hearts, if we pray and ask, He will show us a need in their lives. If a family has children, you shouldn't have to think very hard to come up with a long list of needs where you could be of assistance. A woman with a house full of cherubs is usually pressed for time. Some older women whose children are grown can offer to watch a neighborhood mother's children for an afternoon, just to give her a little time to herself. Can you imagine any greater gift? As a mom, I can't.

> "Anxiety in a man's heart weighs it down, but a good word makes it glad. The righteous is a guide to his neighbor, but the way of the wicked leads them astray."
> —Proverbs 12:25-26

In our society, people are so busy we often don't have time to whip up an extra meal for someone who needs help. But I have a friend who taught me the secrets of advance planning. She keeps at least one, and usually four or five, extra meals in the freezer. Whenever she hears about any kind of family crisis in her area, she is ready—whether it's all the kids in a family coming down with chicken pox, or something more serious.

If she sees a moving van on the block, she quickly appears on the family's doorstep with a meal that she simply had to thaw and warm in the oven or microwave. It is amazing the number of lives that she has touched through such a seemingly insignificant gesture. She uses a helping hand to build relationships over time. When she hosts a witnessing event, like a coffee fellowship, those neighbors are much more willing to attend.

But you don't have to be a great cook to extend kindness. You can offer to take in the mail when people are going out of town, feed their pets or just keep an eye on their house. Be a good neighbor and give people your phone number in case they need someone to check if a light is on or let a repairman in their house.

> "Do not neglect to show hospitality to strangers, for by this some have entertained angels without knowing it."
> —Hebrews 13:2

In the past, when we knew a couple was especially interested in attending a particular event, whether a professional theater production or a sporting event, we have used some of our tithe money to buy tickets and invited them to go with us. We haven't done this very often and you may not agree with this practice. However, occasionally we felt the Lord was showing us we could do something special for somebody that they couldn't afford otherwise. Our purpose was building a relationship for the purpose of ministry.

Some have special gifts in hospitality or flower arranging. Some husbands are great at changing the oil in cars. Maybe they could change the oil in a neighbor's car, especially a single mother's. This is a task that most women have never been educated about and are unlikely to figure out how to do (if they can even find time).

A lot of it is retraining your mind and those of your children to be looking for things that you can do to be available and build relationships with those around you. It is a mind-set. You will be surprised how easy it becomes if you ask the Lord to help you focus on your neighbors. It is so unusual these days for a neighbor to do something with no motive that people just can't believe it.

You will find some who will be sort of suspicious, wondering, *What do they want?* This is why it is extremely important that you not have any personal motive in extending a hand. Don't ever try to sell something to somebody that you're trying to reach. They will quickly feel like a "prospect." Some multilevel marketing schemes have given selling such a bad name that subtle approaches are seldom appreciated. Especially when they follow a supposed free-will gesture.

We have also learned that it is important to try not to raise "Christian issues" with neighbors whom we don't believe know the Lord. In our case, the Lord changed our politics and views on many subjects. But people couldn't have persuaded us.

Tackling controversy as a way of building relationships can raise barriers instead. Even bumper stickers can be a turn-off. I know this is a controversial area, but we feel that having certain bumper stickers—even on issues we feel very passionately about—can ruin our chances of witnessing to a neighbor. Especially if they have already heard something and are eager to stereotype us.

Christians often shy away from getting involved in community activities. We have such limited free time already that sometimes community events pale by comparison. Yet we have seen that getting involved occasionally can also build bridges. As Christians, we are set apart from worldly goals and influences, but we shouldn't be divided from our neighbors. We don't want to give an impression that we think we're better or don't care about them.

> "You are the light of the world. A city set on a hill cannot be hidden; nor does anyone light a lamp and put it under a basket, but on the lampstand, and it gives light to all who are in the house. Let your light shine before men in such a way that they may see your good works, and glorify your Father who is in heaven."
> —Matthew 5:14-16

A certain amount of involvement with your neighbors on issues of local importance can create common ground. When we were living in Atlanta, we got involved in a fight against a proposed highway that was going to run close to our neighborhood. We frankly weren't that concerned about that road. But our neighbors felt so strongly about it that it would have alienated them if we had not given some money to the effort and attended a couple of rallies.

I know a woman who joined her neighborhood baby-sitting coop just to get to know some of the other women around her. I thought that was a great idea—looking for ways she could interact and be a "regular Joe" to people who desperately need the Lord. Too often ordinary folks feel inferior to a famous televangelist or a big-name preacher whose programs are seen by millions. On a day-to-day, down-in-the-trenches basis, who do you think matters more? Someone who flickers across a TV screen occasionally, or someone there to lend a helping hand or a listening ear?

Recently I talked to a couple who became Christians two years ago. Their next-door neighbors were Christians. That couple began praying for them and took one of their children to a vacation Bible school (VBS), where the child became a Christian. The parents were impacted by the change in their child and soon accepted Christ as well. Although their neighbors didn't directly lead them to salvation, simply inviting the child to VBS played a role in their ultimate decision.

An attitude of love and a willingness to open your lives to your neighbors is critical. That helps pave the way. Sooner or later neighbors will ask, "Why are you being so nice to me?" or "What's the reason you're so different?" When that door opens, you want to be prepared to share effectively with them about the source of your love. This is what lifestyle evangelism is all about. It is the kind of lifestyle your children need to grow up with if they are to make an eternal impact.

Questions for Reflection

1. When did you last invite a neighbor over for dinner or socializing? What did you discuss? Explain whether you shared your faith and why (or why not).
2. Have you ever talked to someone whose marriage was falling apart or whose life was filled with personal problems? What kinds of solutions did you offer that person?
3. How would you describe the condition of your family? How do you prepare to welcome guests into your home?

4. List the steps you are taking to prepare your children to be Christian witnesses wherever they go.

5. Describe three ways you can help a neighbor. Set a date in the coming week when you will help by doing one of them.

6. What is the most effective course in evangelism or discipleship you have completed? Why was it helpful to you?

Chapter Twelve
LOVING YOUR HUSBAND

——— Susy Downer

Phil and I are like night and day. As he noted in chapter 3, we attended the same university, same law school, sat side-by-side through the same courses (except "Domestic Relations," which I took to learn how to divorce him); practiced similar legal specialties, accepted Christ the same year, used the same discipleship material and parented the same six children. Yet we remain very different. You may wonder, *Then what hope is there for* our *marriage?*

Don't get discouraged. This is reality. Despite three decades together, a simple question for one of us can represent intense pressure to the other. What one considers an innocent suggestion the other receives as biting criticism. We still harbor differences of opinion on priorities and household finances. In growing closer, we learned our unity means we can more easily hurt each other's feelings. But this isn't cause to give up in disgust or head for divorce court. Growth is painful.

In this chapter I will address five key aspects of growing closer to your husband. However, please encourage your husband to read this chapter too. He needs to know what you are doing to improve your marriage. The goal is to achieve oneness with your husband spiritually, emotionally, volitionally (meaning your will), mentally and physically. These are essentials for every woman who hopes to pass on a godly legacy to her children, grandchildren and future generations.

Spiritual Unity

As we have shared, Phil's struggles with childhood pain and fear, coupled with his Vietnam combat experiences, meant he brought a mountain of anger into our marriage. Ladies, that may not parallel your experience. Your husband may have grown up like I did, in a peaceful home largely absent of conflict and anger. Instead, you may be the one who tends to lash out verbally when under pressure or discouragement.

Whatever side of the anger quotient you are on—and each of us bears some responsibility in the situation—forgiveness is the key. Are you able to forgive even the unforgivable, while simultaneously admitting your own failures?

"Rose," one of the highest-ranking females in her industry, a corporate officer, had been meeting with me to discuss the Bible and spiritual subjects. But after several meetings, it was clear we weren't making progress. Considering what barriers existed in Rose's life, I prayed and asked Phil to set up a meeting with the couple, since he had been counseling her husband on issues of work, setting priorities and his spiritual life.

The four of us met in our office. After an hour of conversation, we were still hearing the cliché, "Everything's fine." But when I asked a fairly pointed question, Rose blurted out that she had been having an affair with a subordinate.

Her husband gasped and broke down in tears. Trying to hide the panic on our faces, Phil and I silently sent up an urgent call to the Lord for wisdom.

I quietly ushered Rose into another room to sort through what had happened and to ask why she had resorted to this action and what she thought God wanted her to do next. Meanwhile Phil tried to console her husband as he lay spread-eagled on the floor, sobbing. About ninety minutes later, Phil and her husband asked us to return. Then Phil and I witnessed something that we will never forget.

Phil had comforted the husband for about an hour and then started reading to him from First Corinthians 13. Known as the "love chapter," it contains a fifteen-point definition of biblical love that has been the framework for our marriage. Although this definition has challenged us every day of our marriage, it has been the underpinning and foundation for a growing, exciting oneness.

When Rose sat down, her husband knelt at her feet. Though in much better control of his emotions, he fought back tears as he confessed how he had not been patient with her and the children. He admitted he had failed to be kind, sweet and gentle and to cherish her. He also listed these faults:

- Being jealous of the time she spent on the job and other activities, which motivated him to ignore her gifts and brag about his own.

- Arrogance for thinking he was right most of the time.

- Being unbecoming in some actions, comments and words, the latter stemming from childhood anger.

- Seeking his own interests, rationalizing that he "deserved a break."

- Failing to forgive her while being provoked too easily.

There were others. Phil and I marveled as we watched the fifteen imperatives of God's love demonstrated through an incredible act of forgiveness. You may wonder why I relate this story, since the husband seems like the one who had to forgive his wife. But at the heart of Rose's actions lay unforgiveness for her husband's many faults.

Not for a minute do I condone what Rose did, nor do I believe that her husband's failures in any way justified hers. However, I do know that two people who are willing to walk with the Lord Jesus Christ in brokenness, forgiveness, confession and love will have a growing, joyful, intimate marriage. Their union will be a living proclamation to the power of Jesus Christ to everyone who crosses their path as it leaves a beautiful legacy for their descendants.

> When it came to displays of anger, I had focused so heavily on Phil's shortcomings in this area I had ignored my own displays of temper. What personal blind spots are you unwilling to admit exist?

Women, are you forgiving your husband for forgetting to hang up his shirts, being harsh with your children, overly involved with work, stubborn or insensitive to your feelings? Forgiveness, reconciliation and love are contagious. As we wives fill ourselves with God's love and forgiveness through a spiritual oneness with Christ, the fullness overflows into our marriage and family.

Not that this is easy to learn. We had years of subtle programming to overcome. Even after Phil became a Christian, it took time for him to subdue his temper. After Christ's peace, love and joy helped him tame that monster, he still struggled. His subtle displays came through tone of voice, body language or demeanor.

However, he wasn't alone. After years of conflict and in reaction to Phil's anger, I also developed a temper. We were a pretty sad (I thought hopeless) match as our explosiveness grated against each other. Finally Phil confronted me and told me to back off. Ironically I had focused so heavily on his shortcomings in this area I had ignored my own. He too recognized that he needed to curb his tendency to erupt when confronted by difficult or painful situations.

Conquering these struggles was the first step toward spiritual unity. We couldn't come together as one during Bible study and prayer if we were tearing into each other the rest of the day. Yet there were many other obstacles, starting with scheduling time that we could spend together with the Lord.

Although we both love reading God's Word, we didn't agree on how to digest it. I nibbled on it throughout the day in addition to listening to a Christian radio program or reading a book. Being more regimented and working outside the home, Phil needed a traditional, early-morning quiet time concentrated on Bible reading, meditation and memorization, and concluding with prayer. To add to the challenge, Phil was a "night" person who liked to stay up late. I went to bed early and arose at the crack of dawn with a burst of energy.

However, as our marriage matured, we reversed roles. To get quiet time, Phil became a morning person and turned in earlier. When the children came along, I stayed up later and later, stealing time alone after putting little ones to sleep. That led to my getting up later each morning, which again put us on separate schedules.

Unintentionally I started encouraging Phil to stay up later, which often resulted in his missing morning devotions and further damaging our relationship. It surfaced through his lack of patience and bad temperament. I will never forget the day when Phil gently but nervously asked me if I knew the biggest block to his essential quiet time.

"No," I replied, looking at him curiously.

"You are," he said.

"Look, this is your problem, not mine," I huffed.

> # God showed me the same solution that applies to so many of our marital disagreements: We had to meet each other somewhere in the middle.

Later, as I reflected on his comment, I recognized that marital unity could include something as simple as going to bed and rising at similar times. Not only could we attune our spiritual lives, but it provided another way of sharing meaningful time. In taking this concern to prayer, God showed me the solution that applies to so many marital disagreements: We had to compromise. Phil stopped casting accusatory glances at me for not getting up quite as early as he did. I recognized that I could just as easily have a quiet time in the morning as late at night.

Sleep was another disagreement. I always seem to need more, so even though we both read the Bible and pray in the morning, we don't get up at exactly the same time. I will never understand how he can have no problem going to bed when he travels alone, yet claims it's impossible for him to sleep when I stay up to tackle my "to do" list. I'll never understand that, but I had to accept this difference.

This may not sound too spiritual, but to achieve spiritual oneness, I learned that every little thing counts. In addition, I came to see that arguing over such matters doesn't help. I also discovered a specific time dedicated to the Lord (with no radio on) is more effective, especially since my days have grown increasingly complex dealing with six children and our ministry of speaking, writing and teaching.

Women, just because you weren't the one who went to war, resulting in damaged emotions, and you have a stable approach to dealing with pressure, doesn't mean you don't need time alone with the Lord. This was the source of contentious discussion, until the day I told Phil I didn't need a quiet time as much as he did. "Well, you may not need one for you," he replied. "But it will help you deal with someone like me. I can always tell the difference when you've been up in the morning praying for me before I start my day."

At first I struggled to accept that. But then I came across Mark 1:35, where Jesus modeled this practice: "In the early morning, while it was still dark, Jesus got up, left the house, and went away to a secluded place, and was praying there."

Praying Together

Another challenge in our marriage was praying together. Though we struggled to establish this habit, I can confidently proclaim the couple that prays together stays together. According to a 1997 Gallup poll, while fifty percent of Christians divorce, only one in 1,154 couples who pray together split apart. Through our experience and discipling other couples, we have observed several aspects of marital prayer that can pose problems.

- Usually one partner is more verbal and comfortable with praying out loud. The other is more sensitive, wanting to express prayers to the Lord quietly and in solitude. Allow for such differences. Don't try to force your partner to do what you do.

- One or both partners may subtly turn prayer into a weapon, asking aloud that God make the other person more patient or see his or her point of view. Never conclude joint prayer time with this kind of request. Lovingly express such thoughts to God in private.

- One partner may be more mature spiritually. After that person has prayed from Genesis through Revelation and covered most of the world's concerns, available time may be gone. Your spouse may feel intimidated. Be sensitive and don't use prayer time to "show off."

> "Devote yourselves to prayer, keeping alert in it with an attitude of thanksgiving; praying at the same time for us as well, that God will open up to us a door for the word, so that we may speak forth the mystery of Christ."
> —Colossians 4:2-3

Here are some suggestions for joint prayer that have worked for us.

1. If one or both of you are hesitant to pray together, resolve to each read a favorite Bible verse. Phil likes Philippians 4:6-7: "Be anxious for nothing, but in everything by prayer and supplication with thanksgiving let your requests be made known to God. And the peace of God, which surpasses all comprehension, will guard your hearts and your minds in Christ Jesus." I like Proverbs 3:5-6: "Trust in the LORD with all your heart and do not lean on your own understanding. In all your ways acknowledge Him, and He will make your paths straight."

After a few days of reading, turn the passages into a prayer. For Philippians, you could pray, "Lord, I know that I'm not supposed to be anxious. You've asked me to take my anxiety to you in prayer, with thanksgiving, and You will return peace. And so, Lord, I just give You the anxious feelings I have about today. In Jesus' name I pray, amen." You can pray such a prayer more than once, then expand it to other areas of life. The important thing is that you both spend about the same amount of time praying.

> It is easy for the more spiritually mature partner in a marriage to hog available prayer time and leave the spouse feeling intimidated. Be sensitive and don't use prayer time to show off superior knowledge and insights.

2. Let the reluctant partner go first. The outgoing one should agree not to pray any longer or more enthusiastically than the reluctant one.

3. Consider praying together after your individual quiet time, but well before each of you needs to start the day's tasks.

4. Commit to pray together for thirty days in a row. According to various experts, this is how long it takes to establish a habit.

5. Strive to mature in prayer so that when you feel the onset of pressure, personal hurt, embarrassment or other setbacks, you aren't afraid to voice your request out loud. Few couples can do this without turning their partner into a "target," but God has used this to reduce tension in our marriage. For example, Phil unintentionally said something that hurt my feelings. Because of other strains that day, I was about to exclaim, "I've had it!" Instead I stopped and prayed, "God, I love this man. He's a wonderful husband. Lord, would You give me a listening ear and a willing heart to understand what it is that Phil is asking or telling me? It's my greatest desire to serve him and You gently and faithfully. Lord, let me be the wife to this husband that You want me to be." Sure enough, God removed the burden.

6. Remember to pray for each other. When Phil is upset or overwhelmed and asks me to pray for him, my response has been like salve for his wounds. Hearing me express my care and concern cheers and encourages him. When he's cranky, I've sometimes thought, *I'll pray for you after you repent,* but fortunately I bit my tongue. Sure, we all get irritated. But I have to remember Christ didn't wait for me to repent before He died for me on the cross. He made the sacrifice first. We are to sacrifice our rights for our spouse.

A Good Report

Another way to build a strong spiritual legacy is to speak approvingly of your mate. The Bible is clear that we are not to gossip, give a bad report, focus on the negative or grumble and complain—especially about those living under the same roof. So often couples voice complaints against each other to their children, which is wrong. It lessens their respect for you and may damage their respect for your partner. Plus children are too young to have to bear such burdens.

Some parents, particularly those whose marriages have split apart, live in fear of their children being turned against them. As an act of self-defense, they excuse their failures by pointing out the other person's. This invariably backfires and sows the seeds of more bitterness. Nor is it necessary. I know this from watching a woman avoid this trap by praising the man who walked away from her to marry someone else.

> "Do all things without grumbling or disputing; so that you will prove yourselves to be blameless and innocent, children of God above reproach in the midst of a crooked and perverse generation, among whom you appear as lights in the world, holding fast the word of life."
> —Philippians 2:14-16

Liane, the woman who discipled me as a young Christian, showed remarkable self-control as she spoke to her children about her ex-husband. During our weekly Bible study prayer sessions, she often cried out to God. She asked Him for grace to be supportive, positive and accurate when talking to her children about her former husband. I marveled at her faith. She had to avoid bitterness and trust that God would honor her prayers and not allow her children to be turned against her.

Year after year, I observed her speak positively about her husband to her children. That resulted in their growing closer to her. They also benefited from a reduction in the tension that inevitably accompanies a divorce. I realized if my friend could be that supportive of her ex-husband, how much more did I need to act that way toward my faithful spouse.

> "He who loves purity of heart and whose speech is gracious, the king is his friend."
> —Proverbs 22:11

Looking back, I see one reason for the peaceful atmosphere in my childhood home was because my mother spoke well of Dad when he was out of town. I never heard her complain, "Well, your father's gone again and I guess he'll probably be late for dinner, so we might as well just go on without him." She was always supportive, talking about how Daddy was working hard for our benefit.

Proverbs 25:11 (KJV) says, "A word fitly spoken is like apples of gold in pictures of silver." Determine to set this kind of picturesque treasure in your home by the words of praise you lavish on your spouse and children.

Emotional Unity

Many of our husbands grew up in an era, or a family, that embraced the Big Lie—namely, the idea that big boys don't cry, feel, touch, get embarrassed or express emotions. Following this misguided philosophy has led to a nation full of husbands who are relatively unemotional. They think that's how they should act.

Granted, God makes some people more concrete in their thinking. They simply don't have the emotional antennae that others (especially women) possess. Whichever side of the spectrum you lean toward, recognize that one blessing of a spouse is helping to balance your emotions. We can work together as one and grasp a more complete picture of life by using our emotions.

One of my failings is a straightforward approach that misses subtle nuances. I assume that what I see is what is there, that what I'm told is everything there is to be expressed and that the past is over and forgotten. Having grown up in a stable, loving home, I have a childhood full of good memories. They don't compare to the kind of challenges Phil faced.

> "Nevertheless, each individual among you also is to love his own wife even as himself, and the wife must see to it that she respects her husband."
> —Ephesians 5:33

As difficult as his dysfunctional home was, he also had to deal with the indignities faced by thousands of 1960s and '70s war veterans. Imagine if we had spit on the New York City firefighters who lost friends, coworkers and loved ones in the September 11, 2001, terrorist attacks. In some respects, that's what Americans did to Vietnam veterans who fought in an unpopular war. Regardless of your views, these men and women answered the call of duty. More than 58,000 lost their lives. Few said "thanks" for their service.

It never occurred to me that I needed to revisit Phil's military service until we met David and Teresa Ferguson,

founders of Intimate Life Ministries. Through their training, I learned to give Phil a special tribute on Veterans Day.
One year I heard popular author Steve Farrar on the radio,
speaking to a stadium packed with men and leading cheers
for those who served in combat in Vietnam. I ran out in the
yard to tell Phil. When he came in, I watched my dear husband weep with appreciation for the cheers he had never received before.

This recognition was also a form of respect, which God
tells us our husbands need (Ephesians 5:33). My problem has
been demonstrating my respect in a way that Phil can sense it.
This is one thing I learned through studying the ten intimacy
needs that Phil reviewed in chapter 7—acceptance, affection,
appreciation, approval, attention, comfort, encouragement,
respect, security, support.

We review this list periodically. I ask Phil how I'm doing
and how I can improve. Through these discussions, I have
learned various ways to communicate my respect. For example, he feels respected when I acknowledge that I need to stick
to my diet so that he doesn't have to work up the courage to
mention it. Or when I'm careful to be punctual for one of his
speaking engagements. He also feels respected when I listen
to one of his stories without interrupting.

This kind of honest evaluation can be scary. The first
time Phil asked me to score him, I asked, "Are you sure?" I
didn't know if he would accept constructive criticism. That
was many years ago, and though this exercise sometimes
causes tender feelings, it has improved our marriage.

Here are some practical guidelines:

- Be "prayed up" and expect to hear some comments
  you may not agree with initially.
- Don't be defensive.

- Listen without interrupting.
- Take notes.
- Be willing to change when your partner truthfully points out a flaw. If you disagree with something, keep quiet and pray about it later.
- After you've had some time to pray and digest the comments, schedule another discussion. If you have had a problem accepting something, explain why. Where you recognize correction is needed, ask what you do that hurts or detracts from a particular need of your spouse and how you can change.

Along the same lines, the Fergusons taught us not to meet emotions with intellect. There is a time for reasoning and a time to repair damage. People with bruised emotions aren't thinking clearly, nor are they too receptive to logical suggestions.

Early in our marriage, one of our worst mistakes when the other felt emotionally hurt or insecure was blurting out some intellectual comment like, "It's not that bad" or "You'll feel better tomorrow." Better to meet emotions with a comforting response. If someone hurts, hurt with him. Comforting each other is a win-win situation. We feel better and are prepared to be more caring in the future.

In emotionally charged situations, avoid generalizations. The use of words like "always" or "never" usually create more conflict. Telling your partner, "You're always insensitive" is inflammatory and denigrates him as a person. If you feel that bad, say, "I feel like you're being insensitive to my feelings right now." Give your husband a chance to comfort you and then discuss how you can reach harmony.

Two Bodies, One Will

Marriage includes melding two wills into one. This includes yielding to the other person, adjusting your schedule to meet others' needs—which always happens with children's activities—and giving up individual rights so your marriage and family will benefit. Too many married couples treat their match as an arrangement of convenience to benefit self. But when couples form a giving partnership, the marriage becomes happier and endures.

I learned about the benefit of flexibility by watching my mother adjust to Dad's schedule, which included travel. In our case, homeschooling gives us more flexibility. Still, I need to mesh activities with Phil's more rigid schedule. After all, nobody else can father my children. As we pass on the legacy of loving one another, we must both have enough time with our kids to provide leadership, interaction, love and support. Because of this, I avoid overscheduling family activities. Even good things can take away the one-on-one time Phil needs with our children.

> Men have weaknesses that are so
> obvious to women that we are
> tempted to continually point out
> irritating traits or complain about their
> conduct. But nagging them generally
> causes more problems and winds
> up being counterproductive.

Another suggestion in helping husbands deal with critical household issues is to prepare them in advance. When they arrive home, they won't feel blindsided. They will have had time to consider a response and ways they can meet a need. I have often done that with a "heads up" through a phone or e-mail message. If Phil has time, he can call home to ask, "How is everyone doing? Who needs some one-on-one time when I get there?"

Naturally, with six children there have been days when I have felt overwhelmed by bad conduct or other disciplinary issues. By alerting Phil, I not only prepare him for the situation but relieve inner stress. However, I have learned to avoid setting certain expectations on how he should handle a situation. Having been away, he has a tough time jumping into disciplinary mode the minute he walks through the door. Keep an open mind and don't try to pour your husband into your mold.

Patience is another quality of joining your will with your spouse's. God defines love as enduring all things (1 Corinthians 13:7). Frankly, some things about our mate take supernatural power to endure. Men have weaknesses that are so obvious to women that we are tempted to continually point out irritating traits or complain about their conduct. However, this usually drives men deeper into a shell, making them less willing to help. Nagging doesn't cure anything.

Sometimes small issues that need correcting can turn into a mountain of conflict when the wife insists on addressing them *right now*. I try to pick a quiet time later when I can discuss something Phil can change to help the family or the closeness of our marriage. Also, I warn him ahead of time and ask him to get "prayed up" before we talk. Here are some other guidelines:

1. I pick a time when we can discuss the issue without feeling rushed.

2. I avoid generalizations by listing specific examples of his behavior.
3. I include some honest compliments so he doesn't feel attacked or degraded.
4. I give him only one or two suggestions at a time.
5. I ask for his suggestions about ways to resolve the dilemma.

If the problem persists, instead of nagging I pray for him. If he agrees with a suggestion I made earlier, I give him time to correct the habit. We will never see eye-to-eye on some things. Take, for example, Phil's tendency to arrive ten to fifteen minutes early whenever we go somewhere. To me that is an utter waste of time. Yet for the most part we have resolved this. When something is vital to him, I do my best to be on time. When I'm under the gun at home, he recognizes he needs to wait patiently while I finish.

We are far from perfect, which means we're still working on our marriage after all these years. It takes considerable prayer, planning and self-discipline to succeed in an intimate relationship.

Being of One Mind

Anyone who has been married knows how easy it is to get cross with each other when we fail to communicate about schedules, issues and important decisions. The following four tips may sound simple, but by failing to follow them millions of marriages haven't lasted until "death do us part."

1. *Prepare for homecomings, key decisions and potential conflicts by holding family business meetings.*

When a husband goes off to work or out of town, he looks forward to coming home. Naturally he expects some peace and rest when he returns. When I know Phil has had a difficult trip, I set aside time for rest just before he comes home so I can offer a willing reception and a listening ear. Over the years I have tried to be more understanding about the pressures he faces. Of course this is a two-way street. We often schedule a "calendar date" so both of us are aware of each other's upcoming activities.

When it comes to various decisions, vacations and holidays, discussing events and plans in advance is invaluable. I compare the twenty-first century to the spin cycle of a washing machine. So much happens in our world that each day's centrifugal force thrusts us apart and squeezes time out of our lives. With proper planning, we can reserve precious moments for reflection, love and communication.

> Women are so intuitive and emotional that we can often expect our husbands to know what we're thinking just by the look on our face. Ladies, men aren't made this way. Just tell them what you're thinking.

2. Read material that will enrich your marriage.

Phil and I love reading books together, particularly about such matters as building intimacy or how to have a more effective prayer life. We also enjoy reading travel guides about a particular location where we plan to go for a weekend break. Most of all, we enjoy reading portions of Scripture to each other and discussing them. We can see God drawing us closer together as we read and meditate on His Word.

3. Don't assume your spouse can read your mind.

Couples (especially women) often make the mistake of thinking their mate knows exactly what they are feeling.

Often I'll be thinking pleasant thoughts about Phil, but because I'm not terribly verbal I'll fail to express them—yet expect him to know I'm admiring him. He prefers verbal praise. I also have to remember that with my husband, once is not enough. He enjoys hearing a compliment two or three times, each phrased a bit differently.

4. Get the facts, ma'am.

While generalizations aren't always true, men tend to be "linear" thinkers. They want to know what is happening and the details of a situation before they decide how to deal with it. Before I approach my husband with an idea or a problem, I try to get all the facts. That improves our communication and understanding.

One Body

Paul wrote in First Corinthians 7:4, "The wife does not have authority over her own body, but the husband does; and likewise also the husband does not have authority over his own body, but the wife does." One of my greatest challenges, and one I believe is common to women, is fully understanding this verse.

Honestly, these words sound good, but they clash with the realities of widely varying schedules, expectations, needs and wants. When we are tired and focused on the needs of our children and a dozen other concerns, it is difficult to serve our husband's needs. Particularly when he seems to have such different appetites. Early in marriage, even discussing intimate matters made me blush.

However, as time passed I gained an appreciation for my role in keeping our marriage intact. He had a goal of staying pure and devoted to our marriage. That made my generosity in our physical relationship an essential element of helping him achieve this goal. Although my shortcomings would not justify his having an affair, I needed to help him avoid undue temptation. Gradually I discovered four ways of helping my husband remain faithful:

1. I can be available for him even when it's not convenient for me.

If we truly have authority over each other's body and I love my husband, I should make sacrifices. Such sacrificial love that helps a marriage endure often begins with sexuality. By sometimes being inconvenienced, we help our husbands avoid temptation. First Corinthians 10:13 says,

> No temptation has overtaken you but such as is common to man; and God is faithful, who will not allow you to be tempted beyond what you are able, but with the temptation will provide the way of escape also, so that you will be able to endure it.

Sometimes the escape is the affection offered by a loving wife.

2. I can recognize my role as a gatekeeper for our home.

Women can flick on the television or keep lingerie catalogs lying around the house and not think a thing of it. For our husbands and maturing sons, however, they can represent the seeds of temptation. Earlier Phil shared the story of how he and our boys were tempted by watching pretty Olympic skaters on television. I almost passed out! (The admission shocked our daughter Abigail too.)

Phil has often said it's the women who turn on the TV, but it's the men who watch it. Judging by what many friends and acquaintances tell me, women like the "company" of TV or radio when they're going through their routine at home. But this can become a deterrent or a trap to our families. Mothers frequently set the home's tone and schedule. If we hope to pass on a godly legacy, our children need to see us modeling prayer, reading the Bible and good literature and listening to good music instead of constantly watching TV or videos.

3. I can get Internet protection.

Millions of good men, including pastors, ministry leaders, businessmen and others, have succumbed to the lure of pornography that is available at the flick of a button. We like a service called CharacterLink. It doesn't simply screen out bad Internet content; it's not a filter that can be circumvented. Instead it restricts viewing of a site until the folks at CharacterLink specifically check it out. This may take a day or two, but with many sites the wait is minimal or nonexistent.

4. I can strive to maintain my figure.

I know women who have lost control of their weight and try to rationalize it with, "My husband's fat too." But you can't control your husband's weight—just yours. This is a painful topic for me, since I have struggled for years with my weight. I wish it weren't important to Phil, but if most men were honest they would admit they wish their wives were slimmer.

While I haven't always been successful, I have been willing to discuss this with Phil, and I'm not going to give up. I share about the struggles I endure, steps I'm taking to try to stay on my diet and confess my failures. In turn, this helps Phil be more open about his failures in bringing home too much work-related tension. Believe me, it's no easier for him to confess this than for me to talk about my weight. This is what being together is all about. It's difficult, but it's worth the price to help our husbands live up to their desire to be a one-woman man.

Such faithfulness is the stuff of lifelong marriages, the kind of marriages that will leave a permanent legacy, blessing your immediate family and rippling throughout society. Regardless of race, economic status, background and social standing, you can have an eternal impact by maintaining a happy, thriving marriage. Even after you vanish from this earth, the ripple effect from that accomplishment will continue.

Questions for Reflection

1. What are the sources of anger in your marriage? How can you resolve them?
2. How often do you read the Bible and discuss it with your mate? How would spending more time in this activity improve your marriage?
3. What changes could you make in your daily schedule to allow more time for prayer with your spouse?
4. How often do you compliment your spouse? Your children? Give two examples.
5. Are you willing to set aside time to grade each other on the ten intimacy needs listed on page 122? Set aside an evening to do that in the coming week.
6. What conflicts in your marriage could be avoided by setting regular meetings to discuss your plans?
7. Tell your mate how you would describe your satisfaction with your marital intimacy. List three ways it could improve.

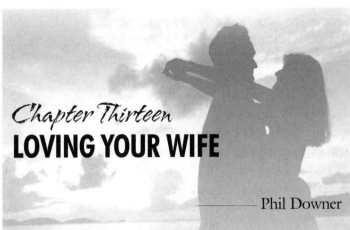

Chapter Thirteen
LOVING YOUR WIFE

———— Phil Downer

Can you imagine a man telling his future bride that sex isn't that important to him—he just wants to be with her? I can hear the men reading this scoffing, "Sure, I can *imagine* him saying it. But I don't believe it." Well, that was exactly what I told Susy when we were dating—and I meant it.

During my younger years, my dating can best be described as a recreational habit, with me at the center. Driven to succeed, I didn't rank marriage a high priority. That is, until I met Susy. Once we fell in love, though, marrying her became just another goal. The prize came at the altar. I believed I had finally found the answer to what many men describe as a "monkey on our backs." Namely, the insatiable appetite for sexual pleasure that increases with feeding. Men, you know this is the truth. So encourage your wife to read this chapter also.

Sex wasn't my only form of medication. I also pursued success, competition and nice things. Yet I was willing to lay it all down for this woman who captivated me. And though I was never more sincere, I was never less capable of meeting this commitment. Since I wasn't a Christian, I put Susy on the throne of my life and expected her to meet the needs only God can. The result? I dearly loved her, but couldn't get along with her.

Without a spiritual dimension, our marriage was doomed. We were dead in our old natures and lacked the power to change. Thank goodness we found the answer in a personal relationship with Christ. As Second Corinthians 5:17 says, "Therefore if anyone is in Christ, he is a new creature; the old things passed away; behold, new things have come."

A friend asked me recently why I have such a passion to speak about the husband-wife relationship, especially since that requires a demanding travel schedule. I mentioned our calling to make disciples, our sense of responsibility to pass on what so many people have modeled for us and our desire to please the Lord. When he pressed for a simpler answer, I replied, "I want everyone in the world to have my marriage. I want everyone in the world to be married to a woman whom Jesus Christ has changed so radically and lives with such a tender boldness that her family and friends call her blessed. I would like my male friends to be as devoted to their wives, and to enjoy being with their wives as much as I enjoy being with mine. I want them to be partners with their spouses in their spiritual lives, family, ministry, work, pleasure and emotional and sexual intimacy."

One of the main reasons we wrote this book was to document for our children the things that we did poorly but which God corrected. In turn, that resulted in the blessings they have enjoyed. Despite our imperfections, foibles and failures, Christ has reigned supreme. We pray every day that our children would have a marriage like ours and learn more about His abundant grace.

About ten years ago, one of our sons said, "Dad, when I'm a father, I'm concerned that I'm going to forget some of the things that you're doing." That was one reason I wrote an earlier book, *A Father's Reward*. It has been the impetus for these final two chapters on the marital aspect of leaving a legacy for your children. Like Susy in the last chapter, I will address the five keys to marital unity in the areas of spiritual, emotional, volitional (the will), mental and physical togetherness.

Spiritual Unity

A vital aspect of spiritual oneness is being equally yoked. If both partners have Christ at the center of their lives, then He is the final authority, power and encouragement instead of two weak, limited humans. The Lord enables two vastly different people to form a common energy, focus and calling for spiritual oneness. Still, evaluating, agreeing on and fine-tuning your spiritual views represents a lifelong endeavor.

> "Do not be bound together with unbelievers; for what partnership have righteousness and lawlessness, or what fellowship has light with darkness?"
> —2 Corinthians 6:14

Like Susy and me, you and your wife have different gifts and goals. For example, Susy felt lukewarm about public speaking, but this is an important part of my calling and skills. Though reluctant initially, she later joined me in addressing couples and families on subjects ranging from discipleship and child-rearing to purity and interpersonal relationships. This is only one of many ways in which we have come together. As we jointly use our gifts and interests, our effectiveness has increased exponentially.

While we are called to make disciples (Matthew 28:18-20), Susy and I are called to both evangelism and discipleship. As we work together to accommodate our gifts and learn to incorporate our children's talents, we are building a stronger legacy for our children.

> "I am sending you to them to open their eyes and turn them from darkness to light, and from the power of Satan to God, so that they may receive forgiveness of sins and a place among those who are sanctified by faith in me."
> —Acts 26:17-18, NIV

We love ministering together and watching various family members take the lead. For example, our son Joshua had a good relationship with his baseball coach. That brought a wonderful man into our lives. I had the privilege of leading him to become a follower of Christ. Today I disciple him one-on-one. This wasn't an overnight process. It required years of prayer, fellowship and fun with the baseball team, the coach and his family.

Here are some thoughts on spiritual oneness that may help your marriage.

1. If one partner is not a Christian, get into a Bible study with another couple or spend time together reviewing the claims of Jesus in the Bible. If neither is possible, the one who knows

Christ as Lord needs to pray for his or her spouse. As you pray, practice lifestyle evangelism. If your actions don't match your words, you won't convince your mate that spending time with God is valuable.

2. If you are both Christians, pray together, attend a biblically based church and follow closely the teaching of a godly pastor.

3. Do "spirit checks" by submitting to each another. This is a rarely used, difficult process. But it will benefit every couple. The problem is that when we follow old habits we don't want to pay attention to the Holy Spirit. Only the Spirit can overcome our impulses, but it takes an act of our will to walk in the Spirit. Sometimes my days seem to be filled with opportunities for correction. I must stop and tell the Lord, or admit to Susy and the children, "I'm going too fast. I'm off His schedule. I'm not operating in His Spirit. I need to take a moment and check my spirit."

Often young Christians memorize Bible verses and seek to follow the directions found in God's Word. But with growth should come the realization that the goal of a Christian is not to operate according to the textbook—it's to let the Master drive the car and do what He wants, how He wants and when He wants by working through us.

While submitting is a challenging discipline, reaching this maturity or even approaching it consistently will reap tremendous returns for your children. Men, what is the leading spiritual lesson that our children need to see in our homes? That as husbands and fathers, we submit to the Lord Jesus Christ. They must see us doing what we are asking them to do.

4. Take regular spiritual inventories. This becomes possible by memorizing the nine fruits of the spirit listed in

Galatians 5:22-23, "But the fruit of the Spirit is (1) love, (2) joy, (3) peace, (4) patience, (5) kindness, (6) goodness, (7) faithfulness, (8) gentleness, (9) self-control."

So often I hear husbands justify harsh attitudes with references to Jesus' indignation over the money changers in the temple. That is simply making excuses for behavior that doesn't demonstrate the fruit of the Spirit. Granted, God gives us permission to defend our families physically and spiritually, even to the point of turning over tables, shooting a wild animal or leaving the presence of profane, uncouth people. Yet these instances are few compared to the Bible verses where He asks us to be as gentle as our Lord and Savior.

> "For the flesh sets its desire against the Spirit, and the Spirit against the flesh; for these are in opposition to one another, so that you may not do the things that you please."
> —Galatians 5:17

Susy can prod me to take a quick spiritual inventory with a simple inquiry like, "Phil, regarding those last words (or actions, or that future step you are contemplating or your intentions) . . . will they fit in one of the nine fruits of the Spirit? If not, why not? Most important, what are you going to do about it?"

One pressure-packed day when I was moving too fast and trying to do too much, Susy confronted me and said, "Phil, you simply can't put pressure on the family the way you are this morning." Shocked, I defended myself with comments about my busy schedule, important deadlines and the critical issues I faced. After listening calmly, she replied, "I understand, but those are not reasons to cause the tension that you are causing in our home."

If I had raised my voice or openly criticized someone, it would have been easier for me to see the problem. But at the moment I felt justified acting this way. You know the feeling—it usually comes in moments of urgency or enormous opportunity. A oneness in the spiritual realm means we allow our partner to confront us with her feelings, not assume that she automatically understands our thoughts and actions.

This weekend on your date, or during a household business meeting, write out the fruits of the Spirit on a sheet of paper. Ranked on a scale of one to ten, discuss how you are doing in living out the fruits of the Spirit in thought, word and deed. A spiritual inventory will help you see where you are compared to the goal of becoming like Jesus to our spouse and children. We want our children to be so excited about Him they would receive Him as Lord and Savior—and pass on their faith from generation to generation.

Emotional Oneness

One of the greatest generals of biblical history was Joshua. A creative, courageous leader, he overcame a powerful enemy. Yet like every leader, he later suffered a great defeat. He faced it with the same courage and faith. He did something that I quit doing at an early age: He wept. Not only did Joshua weep, but he revealed his brokenness, despondency and helplessness to leaders under him.

In chapter 7, I shared about the horror I experienced as a boy when my father introduced me to the woman and children who were supposed to become my new mother and siblings. From that day forth, continuing through the Vietnam War, I kept my boyhood vow to never cry again. Even with my best friend's blood oozing over my hands, I didn't shed a tear. Not much of a legacy to take into a marriage, nor the kind I want to leave my children. It took Christ, God's Word and gut-wrenching effort to release that pain.

The rock-solid, manly resolve that my father taught me worked well in youthful confrontations with bullies, amid combat and during courtroom face-offs. But it doesn't work in marriage, nor with other relationships. It took years to unlearn the past and set a better course for the future. Speaking as a man who has rubbed elbows with thousands of men, I know many of you struggle with the same issues.

> "Then Joshua tore his clothes and fell to the earth on his face before the ark of the LORD until the evening, both he and the elders of Israel; and they put dust on their heads."
> —Joshua 7:6

Let go of that "Rock of Gibraltar" image and express your feelings. I know of many men whose father never, or rarely, said a tender word to them. No matter how good a man Dad was, or what other admirable traits Dad taught them, this lack of emotion left a hole in their souls. Fathers, our sons and daughters are longing for some tenderness from you. They need to know men can be strong and human at the same time.

As Susy mentioned in chapter 12, we need to be willing to comfort our mate and others close to us (though they must be willing to admit the need and willing to receive it). For years I scored a perfect zero in this area. I didn't like to give comfort, nor would I receive it. After all, this practice isn't promoted by government, the military, athletes, the corporate world or the media. Even as Christians, we are keen on setting goals and sharing the gospel with those who don't know Christ. But too often we miss the first, necessary step of loving one another.

> "Remind them to be subject to rulers, to authorities, to be obedient, to be ready for every good deed, to malign no one, to be peaceable, gentle, showing every consideration for all men."
> —Titus 3:1-2

Ministry leaders David and Theresa Ferguson have made a profound impact on us. Some years ago we first had the privilege of attending one of their marriage-intensive sessions. For us, it was invaluable training in expressing and receiving comfort. Not only has this been a huge benefit, but it has been a key in our counseling and discipling other couples. Using their teaching, here are some points that may be helpful in increasing your compassion quotient as a husband:

1. Be willing to comfort others when they express pain by softly speaking words of help instead of instruction. If appropriate, touch them gently while listening carefully to their words.

2. If you cause pain, a biblical confession helps. Something like, "Hey, I'm sorry, but you know I was busy and stressed out" won't sound sincere. Instead, try this: "Honey, please forgive me for being insensitive. When I rescheduled our plans without discussing it with you, my actions lacked respect. I'm very sorry your lovely dinner couldn't be served in a timely way. I know you put excellence into everything you do, especially your gift of hospitality. Again, I was wrong. I put myself first and I want to ask you to forgive me. I will try to be more sensitive in the future."

> "Be anxious for nothing, but in everything by prayer and supplication with thanksgiving let your requests be made known to God. And the peace of God, which surpasses all comprehension, will guard your hearts and your minds in Christ Jesus."
> —Philippians 4:6-7

3. When you have a bad day, your 401-K finishes the year in the basement, your project loses its funding, the car transmission slips into nothingness or you try to handle what three people can't, *stop and recognize that your pain arises from several possibilities*, such as:

- the fear of failure;
- abandonment by people you trusted;
- intense competition at work;
- the pain of exhaustion;
- the pain of criticism;
- the fear of being misunderstood.

Instead of trying to claw your way through the setback, recognize that God has provided a way of being free of that through Scriptures dealing with overcoming fear and anxiety. Then release the emotion caused by the pain and seek comfort. Otherwise it will seep out unexpectedly and harm an innocent party—typically your wife, family or coworkers.

Simply stop, go to your wife and say, "I don't have the energy to discuss all of these issues at this time. I will later, but right now I just need to share with you that this thing that happened, this situation that I'm in, really hurts," and ask her to give you a hug.

> "Speaking the truth in love, we are to grow up in all aspects into Him who is the head, even Christ."
> —Ephesians 4:15

In addition, be willing to tell God how you feel. By expressing fear and pain, you live out Psalm 91:1, which says, "He who dwells in the shelter of the Most High will abide in the shadow of the Almighty." If we verbalize our feelings as we surrender to His rest and (like Joshua) admit we don't have any answers, we demonstrate verse 2: "I will say to the LORD, 'My refuge and my fortress, my God, in whom I trust!'"

The next step is to ask Him to help you. In verse 4, the Lord promised, "[God] will cover you with His pinions, and under His wings you may seek refuge; His faithfulness is a shield and bulwark." *Webster's Dictionary* defines "bulwark" as "a defensive wall or rampart fortification." As I ask for God's help, I have discovered that tears relieve pressure and tension. That brings me great relief and builds emo-

tional oneness with my wife and family. It also demon-
strates real manhood to my children.

4. Our computers have spell-check. *What we as Christians need are word-checks.* A great check comes from Ephesians 4:29, "Let no unwholesome word proceed from your
mouth, but only such a word as is good for edification according to the need of the moment, so that it will give grace
to those who hear."

The problem with most men is that we digest only the
first phrase, "let no unwholesome word proceed from your
mouth." We think, "Well, I don't use four-letter words. I
don't speak in an unwholesome way. I share the truth and
back up my points with Bible verses. I'm not guilty of that.
These people who are offended are just hypersensitive and
need to get a grip on their emotions."

Actually, we need to get a grip on our tongues. As Paul
said a few verses earlier in Ephesians 4:15, we are to speak
truth in love. Sometimes I can speak the truth: "This house
is a mess," but that truth is not accompanied with love.
Sometimes, wanting to be loving, I can avoid confronting
others and ignore failures that should be confronted so they
don't fester, grow and cause division. In that case, I am being kind but not truthful.

The key to a balanced approach comes from Ephesians
4:29: "that it will give grace to those who hear." If people
are not sensing unmerited favor in our words, then perhaps
we are not speaking in an edifying way.

Let me give you an example. Years ago, some good
friends with children in a similar age range called us to
share "some news." Expecting word of another baby, Susy
and I both got on the line. They barely got those words out
of their mouths before we hooted, hollered and celebrated.

Then I piped up, "By the way, after we finish celebrating we really must get going because we are late for the third baseball game of the day. And we're not sure who's got the pizza, the balls and the bats."

About six months later we learned that our reaction proved painful to our young friends. Our handling of the matter didn't feel very loving to them. Our temptation was to brush this off and say, "Well, if you can't celebrate a new baby, what can you celebrate? Besides, how were we supposed to know they weren't completely thrilled about the news?" There was nothing unwholesome about what we said or did. We felt completely justified with our actions. That was the problem! We felt justified, but only because we had not slowed down enough to determine the other couple's feelings.

Such insensitivity will plant the seeds for a lousy marriage, a lousy family and a lousy legacy. As Proverbs 14:12 says, "There is a way which seems right to a man, but its end is the way of death." So often we stand on our "rights," convinced that we are right. We reason, "After all, we're Christians and didn't mean any harm, so how in the world could someone take issue with what we said? We aren't Jesus. We can't be mind-readers."

However, the Holy Spirit can guide us and provide insights into the other person's mind, needs and emotions. The key to Ephesians 4:29 is imparting grace with our words *according to the need of the moment*." In order to determine that, we have to wait, listen, pray and consider the other person's reactions.

Instead of carrying on and talking about our busy Saturday, we could have said to our friends, "Oh, that's wonderful—a new baby. How are you feeling about that?" We would have quickly learned that of course these young parents were celebrating a new creation. But at the time, with a house full of kids, the husband on a new job and the family settling into a new church, the prospects of another, unplanned child seemed overwhelming. Because of the job change, they also faced a lapse in their medical insurance. Plus one of their children had a newly discovered, potentially serious medical condition.

This couple needed a listening ear, a gentle word and a verbal hug. Instead they received a well-choreographed celebration, a statement that we were running late and an abrupt dial tone. Emotional oneness is not just a willingness to share when we hurt each another, but to examine situations where, as a couple, our biases and collective weaknesses inflict pain on others.

Our goal is to build a Christ-centered marriage—and community—where together we encourage one another to love as Jesus did. We want to act through Christ's leading and prosper in our relationships. As Hebrews 10:24-25 puts it, "And let us consider how to stimulate one another to love and good deeds, not forsaking our own assembling together, as is the habit of some, but encouraging one another; and all the more as you see the day drawing near."

Being of One Will

Ever studied your wife? If not, why not? You study your opponent before a court hearing or other adversarial situation, you study a product you hope to sell and you closely examine the car's transmission before getting out your tools and going to work. As husbands, we need to study our wives. How do they do things, and how does that benefit our family, our marriage and the Lord's work?

While modern philosophers have tried to cast men and women as equal—and therefore alike—the latter isn't true. Two sexes mean two natures, as opposite as day and night. Blending them smoothly takes time and effort. Difficulties arise where our wills aren't bad, just different. Typically our differences lead to a contest of wills where one partner tries to convince the other his or her way is best. Often one party gives in, but such begrudging surrenders don't resolve the dispute. Better that we gain mutual encouragement, complement each other and help each other deal with our weaknesses. Sometimes that calls for waiting and praying about the disagreement instead of seeing who can win the match.

> "Let all bitterness and wrath and anger and clamor and slander be put away from you, along with all malice. Be kind to one another, tender-hearted, forgiving each other, just as God in Christ also has forgiven you."
> —Ephesians 4:31-32

This kind of mutual admiration should do away with the all-too-common criticism, sour sarcasm, cutting jokes and snide remarks about men-vs.-women matchups. Such comments are not edifying or unifying and fail to leave a good impression on our children. This is not the kind of legacy they need to carry into their marriages. You know why millions of young adults aren't married today? It's because most of them don't want the marriage their parents had. Do your children want the marriage that you have? Do they see two people working together or two independent people negotiating as if they were parties to a lawsuit?

Granted, sometimes negotiations are necessary, especially on issues of lasting disagreement. For example, Susy and I will go to the grave differently. If she goes first, leaving me in charge, there is no doubt everyone will be on time. In fact, I will have made very sure that our family will show up early. I will probably have broken off several conversations (a bit curtly too) to be sure that I've reviewed the checklist for the fourth time. Someone will be a little hurt that he didn't get to offer his input on a favorite hymn for the service.

At my funeral, the limousine will undoubtedly arrive late. The corner of Susy's black dress will be caught in the door. The odds are nine out of ten that someone will be eating macaroni in the family limo. There will be plenty of time for people to talk. Though little will be done in a timely manner, no one will feel rushed. And I can hear Susy whispering to my lifeless form as she bends over the casket, "Wait a minute. What's the hurry?"

The point is, how will we live together while we're still alive? The answer is that we want to operate the way Jesus desires, with patience, understanding and a willingness to bend our preferences for the other's benefit. Being of one will doesn't mean trying to become a mirror image of your partner, since that will never happen anyway. But like a hand slipping into a glove, we don't endlessly quarrel over our differences. Instead, we prefer the warmth we provide for each other.

Being of One Mind

Many years ago my combat buddy, Ralph, and I stood on the side of a hill and sprang a surprise attack on a line of

North Vietnamese soldiers traversing through the valley below us. Firing more than 500 rounds a minute, our machine gun rained a torrent of lead and steel on the enemy column. Though they were relieved when our gun jammed, we were mortified. Their return fire crackled in our ears, making us feel like we had been tossed into a popcorn popper.

There we stood, as opposite as any married couple. Ralph was an African-American, streetwise urbanite, I, a white, suburban greenhorn who thought "soul" was what went on the bottom of a shoe. Yet we shared a common goal of survival and protecting the comrades who depended on our machine gun fire. We cleared the gun in about fifteen seconds and returned fire. When the smoke cleared, we hadn't lost a man.

> "All Scripture is inspired by God and profitable for teaching, for reproof, for correction, for training in righteousness; so that the man of God may be adequate, equipped for every good work."
> —2 Timothy 3:16-17

We cleared the machine gun because we had the courage to stand together. Since I didn't know the Lord then, I didn't credit His sovereignty. In my mind, we survived because of our expert training and memorizing the manufacturer's handbook. We knew exactly what to do. Having practiced often, we knew how to dismantle that gun and clear it despite enemy fire hailing down around us.

Likewise, for marriages not only to survive but to thrive and leave a shining legacy, we must know God's instruction

manual. Reading the Bible, hearing sermons from it, singing about it and meditating on its truths are all wonderful.
But as couples we must roll up our sleeves, dig in, study and
memorize His Word.

When the end of our earthly day comes and we rejoice
with Christ for eternity, I want our children to say that they
saw their mom and dad set their hearts on learning God's
Word and His ways. I want them to recall that we tried to
become more and more like Him each day. I want them to
say that by our watching the truths of Christ which we
cherished in our hearts, they saw Jesus modeled before
them and thereby learned His character, presence, provi-
sion, point of view, purposes and peace. When we blend
our minds with Christ's, we become of one mind.

> "For Ezra had set his heart to study the law
> of the LORD and to practice it, and to teach
> His statutes and ordinances in Israel."
> —Ezra 7:10

The Old Testament prophet Ezra left a legacy with the
people who followed after him. That is the same kind of legacy we want to leave with our children. But it only comes
from meditating on and memorizing His Word, studying its
meaning and applications and digging deep into the mind of
Christ.

In the frantic-paced world in which we live, this may
sound impossible. Not true. Try taking a three-by-five index card, writing a verse on it and digging into the meaning
of each word. Carry the card with you, memorize the verse
and make it as familiar as your home address. Teach it,

chew on it, meditate on it. Then take another card and repeat the process.

In church, don't just listen to the sermon. Jot down some key points from the message. Grasp the thoughts and truths in it. Get a new Bible and commit to read several chapters a day with the goal of reading through it in a year. Don't just sniff at the Word, or lick at it or chew a tiny morsel. Be like Jeremiah, who said he ate it: "Your words were found and I ate them, and Your words became for me a joy and the delight of my heart; for I have been called by Your name, O LORD God of hosts" (Jeremiah 15:16).

Physical Togetherness

According to First Corinthians 6:16, Susy and I are one body, but I still like hers best. Years ago I vowed to live as a one-woman man and to teach my sons the same. In a world filled with sexual temptation and the popular rationalization that "everyone does it," adhering to this principle isn't easy. Yet it never has been. Why else did my hero, King David, stumble because of lust? God called David a man after His own heart. But he was also a man after his neighbor's wife. (You can read the story in Second Samuel 11.) How can this be? To paraphrase a Scripture, "None is safe; no, not one."

David was in the wrong place at the wrong time. Instead of going off to war, he stayed at home, where he fell to temptation. Likewise for us today. Men, one of the worst things you can do is spend an extra night in a strange city to save a couple hundred bucks on plane fare. Or take an afternoon off on an out-of-town trip without telling anyone where you're headed. It is so easy to end up in the wrong place at the wrong time.

Does your wife know the truth about your desires? One of the best things you can do is come clean and tell her how you feel. Let her know that to you, a Victoria's Secret catalog isn't about lingerie, it's pornographic. If you don't want to go to the beach because you know there will be too much skin on display, tell her. She won't mind doing something else instead. Don't rationalize that a little looking never hurt. Such so-called innocence can destroy a relationship.

> "You have heard that it was said, 'YOU SHALL NOT COMMIT ADULTERY'; but I say to you that everyone who looks at a woman with lust for her has already committed adultery with her in his heart."
> —Jesus in Matthew 5:27-28

Recently Susy and I sat with a couple and listened to the wife pour out her feelings about how her heart had been torn apart by her husband's unfaithfulness. Shocked and defensive, he posed some good arguments—until we realized it wasn't what he was *doing*, it was what he was *looking at*. And when. His wife got so upset with his ogling shapely young women in the mall and at dinner that she dreaded going out. Her husband had set an impossible standard for her to meet.

Even when she reached her wedding-night target weight, her husband's eyes left home continually. Feeling unwanted and undesirable, she drifted away emotionally and became uninvolved in their times of intimacy. This caused her husband to be increasingly dissatisfied, which increased his potential for using pornography. Once they reached this mutual stage of dissatisfaction, the end was near. Their hearts were being drawn apart by something neither had set out to do or intended. Neither would have dreamed this would ever happen to them.

Some men are more affectionate and relational than their wives. They aren't as likely to get involved in visual straying, but rather in an attachment to feelings. I once worked with a man whom I got to know well. He continually counseled women in his office who were going through job, health or family struggles. Over time, he became the office "ear"—and "heart." Though seeming to be a perfect family man after business hours, I concluded he wasn't faithful emotionally to his spouse. His intimate discussions with coworkers initiated a slow process of giving away his innermost affections.

Are you doing the same? When you get up in the morning and get dressed for a big day at the office, do you wear certain things depending upon what female you'll see that day? If so, you may be giving away your heart. Do you drive through the bar district to catch a glimpse of the activity? You are giving away your heart. Eyeing women on the street? You are teaching your daughters that what matters is the way they look, not what they are in Christ. And you are leaving your wife with a deep sense of insecurity that sometimes she's not able to express.

To conclude this section, here are ten suggestions for being a one-woman man.

1. When you are out of town or alone, open up the Bible and read some verses after placing a picture of your family nearby. In your mind, envision your kids sitting on the corner of your bed, smiling and saying, "That's my Dad."

2. Avoid private temptations that go along with fantasizing a sexually intimate physical act.

3. Maintain a close friendship with someone who knows something about your life and will ask you tough questions. Treat accountability as more than meeting a perfunctory checklist.

4. Don't look at skin. I've decided I'm just not competent around naked women, whether in TV and movies or on billboards and the beach. If we're at a crowded sunbathing beach, my sons and I avoid afternoon heat and skimpy suits.

5. Express to your wife that you are visual and convince her you need to enjoy her body. Satan spends a lot of time trying to make men imagine that what's covered up has a great deal of variance. Actually God made bodies quite similar.

6. Avoid things that break down your self-control. As a new Christian, I realized one or two glasses of wine ruined my self-control when it came to sexual purity—looking, joking, fantasizing. When pouring a glass of wine at his house recently, a friend said, "Oh that's right, you don't drink. That's funny, because that was Christ's first miracle." I thought, *That may be true, but Jesus held His wine better than I did.*

7. Ask friends and business colleagues who are going out what they plan to do, then find a way to provide your own transportation. Too many men get caught with the "crowd" and give in to peer pressure in unsafe places.

8. Carefully explain to your wife that you have different needs than hers, and while you're willing to recognize hers, she needs to recognize yours. Tell her, "I need you to understand this difference, in the same way that you're more emotional." However, neither should you place unrealistic expectations on your wife.

9. Build a legacy through a good report. Don't brag about the young female at work who "has a great mind." Don't be sarcastic about your mate or criticize her in front of the children. Women have left their homes and families by the droves because those who benefit most from their service don't thank, appreciate, respect or encourage them. If your wife is at home, tell your children she could go off and get a great job, make a lot of money and buy a new dress, but instead she is investing in the family. If your wife works, make her homecoming the most joyful event of her day.

10. Be the spiritual leader at home. Whether your home turns in the direction of grumbling and discontent or joy and appreciation depends on your attitude. Your wife may be equally competent or more biblically astute, but God called men to be spiritual leaders. Don't shirk the task. In which direction are you leading your family? As I conclude this book, here is a checklist for you to consider:

1. Who's the first to pray in your house when there's conflict?
2. Who's the first to say "I'm sorry" when there's a disagreement?
3. Who pouts the most?
4. Who does the freeze out/quiet/I'm fine routine?
5. Who leaves the home in frustration from time to time?
6. Who raises his or her voice when a gentle answer turns away wrath?
7. Who is the first one to do Bible study in the morning?
8. Who leads the charge to church, to Bible study or to have the neighbors who are contemplating a divorce over?
9. Who is discipling someone down the street?
10. Who has the greatest insight as to what the pastor was getting at with the sermon?
11. Who listens to Christian radio? Who turns the conversation away from the antics of people who are paid to play to the truths of our Lord that bring great eternal payoffs?

12. How many qualities do you have that are identified by your daughter as ones she wants in a husband?

13. Who is more concerned about how he or she acts, looks and sounds outside the home as compared to inside the home?

Every man and woman wants to leave a legacy. And there is no better way to do that than to have a family that God will use to raise and disciple competent, capable, high-charactered and godly young people to carry on our mission and values. This challenge can be overwhelming, yet applying the practical steps and biblical truths of this book in bite-sized pieces is not only achievable, but desirable and essential in leaving the legacy we all desire.

Questions for Reflection

1. How would your children describe your marriage? If you're feeling courageous, ask them.

2. How are you and your spouse working together to advance God's kingdom?

3. Men, how would your children describe you as a spiritual leader? How often do you pray with them?

4. Men, when is the last time you showed emotion (other than anger) in your home?

5. What kind of tenderness did your father display? How has that affected your life?

6. Can you recall a time when your words hurt your mate? How did you resolve the problem?

7. Does your spouse understand your sexual feelings? When is the last time you talked about this subject?

Contact the Authors

To discuss a conference, retreat or church event, Phil can be reached at 423.886.6362 or at phildowner@DNAministries.org. For information about this and other books by the Downers, video or audio series, a calendar of events, references and endorsements or the Downer family, please check the DNA Web site at www.DNAministries.org.

Helpful Resources

CharacterLink: www.characterlink.com, 888.330.8678. CharacterLink offers outstanding computer protection from pornographic and other objectionable Internet sites.

Child Evangelism Fellowship (CEF): www.cefonline.com, 800.300.4033. CEF provides excellent training materials for setting up Good News Clubs in your home or other proven methods for evangelizing and discipling children.

CBMC (Christian Business Men's Committee): www.cbmc.com, 800. 566.2262. CBMC publishes both Operation Timothy discipleship material and the Living Proof video series, *Lifestyle Evangelism* and *Lifestyle Discipleship*.

Crown Ministries: www.crown.org, 800.722.1976. The purpose of Crown Ministries is to teach God's people financial principles. They have wonderful resources for adults and children.

Discipleship Journal **Bible Reading Plan:** www.navpress.com. Two different plans for reading the Bible through in a year are offered.

Discipleship Network of America: www.DNAministries.org, 432.886. 6362. DNA's vision is to win and disciple people to become disciple-makers. This is accomplished through marriage and family conferences, men's retreats, homeschool and church events, books and tapes.

Family Life: www.familylife.com, 800.358.6329. Family Life has a goal of saving marriages and families and provides excellent resources to support its vision.

Focus on the Family: www.family.org, 800.232.6459. Focus on the Family has an outstanding breadth of resources to assist in every kind of family issue.

Institute in Basic Life Principles (IBLP): www.iblp.org, 630.323.9800. IBLP is dedicated to strengthening families. Their seminars have blessed millions.

Intimate Life Ministries: www.GreatCommandment.net, 800.881.8008. Intimate Life Ministries is a training and resource ministry whose purpose is to assist in the development of Great Commandment ministries worldwide. Their marriage intensives are life-changing.

Revive Our Hearts: www.reviveourhearts.com, 877.432.7894. Revive Our Hearts is the radio Bible teaching ministry of Nancy Leigh DeMoss, who has a deep burden for genuine revival among women.

Ronald and Judy Blue: www.ronblue.com/resources_books.html, 800. 841.0362. Ron and Judy have written *Raising Money-Smart Kids* and many other financial resources.

Stories of Great Christians, Moody Audio Ministry: www.mbn.org, 800.626.1224. Audio tapes on the lives of outstanding role models in Christian history are offered.

Your Story Hour: www.yourstoryhour.com, 800.987.7879. Audio recordings of more than 500 stories taken from Scripture, literature, history and everyday life teach character qualities while they entertain and inspire.

Youth With A Mission (YWAM): www.ywam.org, 888.926.6397. YWAM offers a Personal Prayer Diary Daily Planner.